Shhh!
The Sound of Sheer Silence

Shhh!
The Sound of Sheer Silence

A Biblical Spirituality that Transforms

MARK G. BOYER

WIPF & STOCK · Eugene, Oregon

Wipf & Stock
An Imprint of Wipf and Stock Publishers
199 W. 8th Ave., Suite 3
Eugene, OR 97401

www.wipfandstock.com

PAPERBACK ISBN: 978-1-5326-7969-8
HARDCOVER ISBN: 978-1-5326-7970-4
EBOOK ISBN: 978-1-5326-7971-1

Manufactured in the U.S.A.   02/18/19

Dedicated to the
Sisters of Charity of the Incarnate Word
who came from St. Joachim Parish,
Old Mines, Missouri:
Sister Loraine Bourisaw, CCVI;
Sister Marie Coleman, CCVI;
Sister Yvonne DeGonia, CCVI;
Sister Dorothy Mary Politte, CCVI;
Sister Rose Mary Politte, CCVI.

"A certain amount of silence and solitude is necessary for any appreciation of the sacred."

—JOHN GARVEY

"There is nothing so much like God in all the universe as silence."

—MEISTER ECKHART

The word LISTEN has the same letters as the word SILENT!

"How good it is to center down! To sit quietly
and see one's self pass by!"

—HOWARD THURMAN

"… [G]o into your room and shut the door and pray to your Father who is in secret; and your Father who sees in secret will reward you."

—MATT 6:6

Contents

Abbreviations | viii
Notes on the Bible | xi
Introduction | xv

1 **Silence** | 1
   Primeval Silence | 1
   Silence! | 2
   Keep Silence | 3
   Not Keep Silence | 4
   There was Silence | 5
   Wait in Silence | 7
   Kept Silence | 8
   Learn in Silence | 9
   Sit in Silence | 10
   Motion for Silence | 11
   Miscellaneous Silence | 12

2 **Silent** | 14
   Be Silent! 1 | 14
   Be Silent! 2 | 15
   Not Be Silent | 16
   Keep Silent! 1 | 17
   Keep Silent! 2 | 18
   Not Keep Silent | 19
   Silent Like Sheep | 20

Are Silent | 22
Was Silent | 23
Were Silent | 24
Wisely Silent | 25
Remain Silent | 26

3 **Quiet** | 28
Be Quiet! 1 | 28
Be Quiet! 2 | 29
Be Quiet! 3 | 31
Keep Quiet | 32
Quiet and Peace | 33
Quiet Land | 34
Quiet People | 35
Quiet City | 36
Quiet | 38
Not Quiet Sea | 39
Quiet Spirit | 40

4 **Still and Calm** | 42
Be Still, Be Calm | 42
Dead Calm | 43
Keep Still | 44
Stand Still 1 | 46
Stand Still 2 | 47
Silent and Still | 49
Sit Still, Lie Still | 50
Still Sun and Moon | 51
Calm and Still | 53
Calm Harbor, Still Waters | 54
Calm Anger and Wrath | 56
Hush | 57

5 **Transfigured by Silence** | 59
Transfiguration according to Mark | 60
Transfiguration according to Matthew | 62
Transfiguration according to Luke | 63

Others Transfigured by Silence | 64
Application | 67

Bibliography | 69
Recent Books by Mark G. Boyer | 71

Abbreviations

BCE = Before the Common Era (same as BC = Before Christ)
CB (NT) = Christian Bible (New Testament)
    Acts = Acts of the Apostles
    Col = Letter to the Colossians
    1 Cor = First Letter of Paul to the Corinthians
    Gal = Letter of Paul to the Galatians
    Heb = Letter to the Hebrews
    John = John's Gospel
    Luke = Luke's Gospel
    Mark = Mark's Gospel
    Matt = Matthew's Gospel
    1 Pet = First Letter of Peter
    2 Pet = Second Letter of Peter
    Phil = Letter of Paul to the Philippians
    Rev = Revelation
    Rom = Letter of Paul to the Romans
    1 Thess = First Letter of Paul to the Thessalonians
    1 Tim = First Letter to Timothy
    Titus = Letter to Titus
CE = Common Era (same as AD = *Anno Domini,* in the year of
    the Lord)
cf. = confer, compare

HB (OT) = Hebrew Bible (Old Testament)

Amos = Amos

1 Chr = First Book of Chronicles

2 Chr = Second Book of Chronicles

Dan = Daniel

Deut = Deuteronomy

Ecc = Ecclesiastes

Esth = Esther

Exod = Exodus

Ezek = Ezekiel

Gen = Genesis

Hab = Habakkuk

Isa = Isaiah

Jer = Jeremiah

Job = Job

Jonah = Jonah

Josh = Joshua

Judg = Judges

1 Kgs = First Book of Kings

2 Kgs = Second Book of Kings

Lam = Lamentations

Lev = Leviticus

Mal = Malachi

Neh = Nehemiah

Prov = Proverbs

Ps(s) = Psalm(s)

1 Sam = First Book of Samuel

2 Sam = Second Book of Samuel

Zech = Zechariah

Zeph = Zephaniah

NABRE = The New American Bible Revised Edition

OT (A) = Old Testament (Apocrypha)

Add Esth = Additions to Esther

2 Esd = Second Book of Esdras

1 Macc = First Book of Maccabees

2 Macc = Second Book of Maccabees

3 Macc = Third Book of Maccabees

4 Macc = Fourth Book of Maccabees

Sir = Sirach (Ecclesiasticus)

Tob = Tobit

Wis = Wisdom (of Solomon)

Notes on the Bible

THE BIBLE IS DIVIDED into two parts: The Hebrew Bible (Old Testament) and the Christian Bible (New Testament). The Hebrew Bible consists of thirty-nine named books accepted by Jews and Protestants as Holy Scripture. The Old Testament also contains those thirty-nine books plus seven to fifteen more named books or parts of books called the Apocrypha or the Deuterocanonical Books; the Old Testament is accepted by Catholics and several other Christian denominations as Holy Scripture. The Christian Bible, consisting of twenty-seven named books, is also called the New Testament; it is accepted by Christians as Holy Scripture. Thus, in this work:

—Hebrew Bible (Old Testament), abbreviated HB (OT), indicates that a book is found both in the Hebrew Bible and the Old Testament;

—Old Testament (Apocrypha), abbreviated OT (A), indicates that a book is found only in the Old Testament Apocrypha and not in the Hebrew Bible;

—and Christian Bible (New Testament), abbreviated CB (NT), indicates that a book is found only in the Christian Bible or New Testament.

In notating biblical texts, the first number refers to the chapter in the book, and the second number refers to the verse within the chapter. Thus, HB (OT) Isa 7:11 means that the quotation comes from Isaiah, chapter 7, verse 11. OT (A) Sirach 39:30 means that the quotation comes from Sirach, chapter 39, verse 30. CB

(NT) Mark 6:2 means that the quotation comes from Mark's Gospel, chapter 6, verse 2. When more than one sentence appears in a verse, the letters a, b, c, etc. indicate the sentence being referenced in the verse. Thus, HB (OT) 2 Kgs 1:6a means that the quotation comes from the Second Book of Kings, chapter 1, verse 6, sentence 1. Also, poetry, such as the Psalms and sections of Judith, Proverbs, and Isaiah, may be noted using the letters a, b, c, etc. to indicate the lines being used. Thus, Psalm 16:4a refers to the first line of verse 4 of Psalm 16; there are two more lines of verse 4: b and c.

There may be a difference in the verse numbers between the New Revised Standard Version (NRSV) and the Vulgate (the Latin translation of the Septuagint, such as *The New American Bible Revised Edition* [NABRE]). This is true particularly with the Psalms, but with other books as well. Thus, NRSV Isaiah 9:2–7 is NABRE (Vulgate) Isaiah 9:1–6; NRSV Isaiah 9:2–4, 6–7 is NABRE (Vulgate) Isaiah 9:1–3, 5–6. Introductory material to Bibles usually indicates which verse-numbering is being used.

In the HB (OT) and the OT (A), the reader often sees LORD (note all capital letters). Because God's name (Yahweh or YHWH, referred to as the Tetragrammaton) is not to be pronounced, the name Adonai (meaning *Lord*) is substituted for Yahweh when a biblical text is read. When a biblical text is translated and printed, LORD (cf. Gen 2:4) is used to alert the reader to what the text actually states: Yahweh. Furthermore, when the biblical author writes Lord Yahweh, printers present Lord GOD (note all capital letters for GOD; cf. Gen 15:2) to avoid the printed ambiguity of LORD LORD. When the reference is to Jesus, the word printed is Lord (note capital L and lower case letters; cf. Luke 11:1). When writing about a lord (note all lower case letters (cf. Matt 18:25) with servants, no capital L is used.

Presuppositions

The HB (OT) begins as stories passed on by word of mouth from one person to another. Sometime during the oral transmission stage, authors decide to collect the oral stories and write them. A change occurs immediately. One does not tell a story the same way one writes a story. Repetition and correction occur in oral story-telling. Except for future emendations by copyists, single statements by characters and plot structure guides dominate written stories. Furthermore, in both oral and written story-telling, types or models are employed. For example, in the CB (NT) Jesus becomes a type of Moses in Matthew's Gospel. When orally narrating or writing a story, the teller or author consciously creates one character as a type of another in order to make the character and his or her words and actions intelligible to the originally intended hearer or reader.

In the CB (NT) the oldest gospel is Mark's account of Jesus' victory. The author of Matthew's Gospel copied and shortened about eighty percent of Mark's material into his book and then added other stories to make the work longer. The author of Luke's Gospel copied and shortened about fifty percent of Mark's material into his orderly account and then added other stories to make the work much longer. Mark's Gospel begins as oral story-telling, lasting for about forty years in that form. An unidentified author, called Mark for the sake of convenience, collects the oral stories, sets a plot, and writes the first gospel around 70 CE. Because Jesus was expected to return soon, no one had thought about recording what he had said and done until Mark came along and realized that he was not returning as quickly as had been thought. About ten years after Mark finished his gospel, Matthew needed to adopt Mark's narrative—originally intended for a peasant Gentile readership—to a Jewish audience. And about twenty years after Mark finished his gospel, Luke needed to adapt Mark's poor Gentile-intended work for a rich, upper class, urban, Gentile readership. The author of John's Gospel did not know the existence of the other three works collectively named synoptic gospels.

Furthermore, gospels were not first intended to be read privately as is done today. They were meant to be heard in a group. The very low rate of literacy in the first century would have never dictated many copies of texts since most people could not read, and their standard practice was to listen to another read the stories to them. Thus, what began as oral story-telling passed on by word of mouth became written story-telling preserved in gospels. A careful reading of Mark's Gospel will reveal the orality still embedded in the text, especially evident in the repetition of words (like immediately) and the organization of stories in three parts. In rewriting Mark, Matthew and Luke remove the last traces of oral story-telling.

Introduction

This Book

The title of this book is *Shhh! The Sound of Sheer Silence.* The *Shhh!* part of the title represents the sound a person makes when he or she wishes another to be silent or quiet. The sound is usually accompanied with the gesture of the pointer finger—the finger closest to the thumb on either hand—being placed vertically over one's mouth. *The Sound of Sheer Silence* part of the title comes from the HB (OT) First Book of Kings. Once the prophet Elijah ascends Mount Horeb (Sinai), he witnesses "a great wind, so strong that it was splitting mountains and breaking rocks in pieces before the LORD, but the LORD was not in the wind; and after the wind an earthquake, but the LORD was not in the earthquake; and after the earthquake a fire, but the LORD was not in the fire; and after the fire a sound of sheer silence" (1 Kgs 19:11b–12). It is in Elijah's experience of the sound of sheer silence that he encounters the LORD. What escapes many readers of that biblical text is its oxymoronic character. The LORD makes his presence known in the sound of sheer silence. The words *sound* and *silence* are contradictory; thus, they form an oxymoron. One cannot have the *sound* of silence (since silence by definition is the opposite of sound); neither can one have *silent* sound (since sound by definition eliminates silence). Nevertheless, that is how Elijah experiences the divine presence. Garvey says that "silence speaks to us."[1] The "sense of the deep silence and mystery of things"[2] occurs in solitude. "A certain amount of silence and solitude is necessary for any appreciation of the sacred," states Garvey.[3]

The subtitle of this book is *A Biblical Spirituality that Transforms*. The forty-six entries are based on biblical material that is divided into four chapters: (1) Silence, (2) Silent, (3) Quiet, and (4) Still and Calm. The last chapter presents biblical reflections on how a person is transfigured by silence. Thus, the source of spirituality for this book is the Bible.

The word *spirituality* is formed from the word *spirit*. It means the fact or condition of being spirit, and it refers to that aspect each person shares—that invisible nature some call being, essence, breath, wind, etc. Since all people participate in the spirit that animates all—a universal spirit—spirituality results from connecting the individual spirit through reflection, meditation, and contemplation to the universal Spirit all share. That is why Meister Eckhart can declare, "There is nothing so much like God in all the universe as silence."[4] The psalmist sings, "For God alone my soul waits in silence" (Ps 62:5).

According to Shapiro, spirit is one of five dimensions in which we live—body, heart, mind, soul, and spirit—of which "only spirit is birthless and deathless."[5] That is why many people practice a spirituality, a way of life, a way of living now that nourishes the individual spirit connected to the great Spirit with whom we become one gradually in this life and which becomes total on the other side of death. It is the Spirit who gives life to all things, making them holy, and drawing all spirits together into one. Each person

1. Garvey, *Wonder*, 4.
2. Ibid.
3. Ibid.
4. "Meister Eckhart," AZQuotes.com.
5. Shapiro, "Roadside Assistance," 19.

embodies and expresses Spirit. Most history of spirituality records attempts by people to get out of this world into a transcendent one in the divine presence. This escapist spirituality misses the point that the divine is both transcendent and imminent. God chose incarnation, enfleshment, embodiment because "Spirit always desires to incarnate itself. Matter always wants to be God."[6] Spirituality is about our connection to the divine here and now and on the other side of death. Getting to heaven, in popular language, is based first on getting to earth. That's what incarnation did—wed heaven to earth. Developing a spirituality of silence enables the individual spirit on earth to connect to the divine Spirit in heaven now. ". . . [T]he breath breathed into [us] at birth returns at death to the One who breathes it."[7]

Thus, the transformation that occurs to us through silence here and now is an experience of what awaits us after the last transfiguring experience of our lives: death. Shapiro refers to Thomas Keating who said that dying is an extension of living.[8] We are so much more than who we think we are. During times of silence and quiet, we can experience spirit connected to Spirit, and we know that the body, heart, mind, and soul—"the dimension of interbeing where [we] realize that each happening is a happening of the singular happening [we may] call God"[9]—all die. In deep silence, we recognize that all things have soul, in Shapiro's words, "they inter-are."[10] But soul is not spirit. Spirit is "the infinite, fluid, and non-dual process of . . . happening in, with, as, and beyond all finite happenings."[11] It is the awareness from silence of the birthless and deathless spirit (Spirit) that is all—pure being, pure consciousness, pure bliss[12]—into which death transfigures us.

6. Rohr, "Ascending," 1.

7. Shapiro, "Roadside Assistance," 20.

8. Ibid.

9. Ibid.

10. Ibid.

11. Ibid.

12. Ibid.

Using This Book

This book is designed to be used by individuals for private study and prayer. The goal of this book is to foster a spirituality of silence as it flows from the Bible.

A five-part exercise is offered for the entries in all four chapters.

1. **Title**: A one- or two-word title is given to the entry. Not only does the one-or two-word title give focus to the entry, but it imitates *Lectio Divina* (Divine Reading), the practice of reading a biblical passage and choosing a word from it for reflection, meditation, and prayer. *Lectio Divina* promotes communion with God through reflection on God's Word (Jesus Christ) and God's word (Bible). Traditionally, *Lectio Divina* has four separate steps: read, reflect, journal/meditate, and pray or contemplate.

   The one-word title is designed to promote mindfulness. According to Annemarie Scobey:

   > Mindfulness is the practice of maintaining a moment-by-moment awareness of thoughts, feelings, the body, and the surrounding environment. A person who tries to be mindful focuses on what he or she senses and feels in the present moment rather than thinking about what might need to be done later or returning to a memory. Mindfulness is the opposite of multitasking. Mindfulness is truly listening, fully tasting, deeply experiencing; it's taking our feelings as they come and not burying them or pushing them away.[13]

2. **Scripture**: A verse or two from Scripture is presented to illustrate the aspect of biblical silence under consideration. Garvey states, "We need words, but we need them to take us to the place where we realize their inadequacy."[14] The place where we read the biblical verse(s) must be silent, accord-

---

13. Scobey, "Keep Prayer in Mind," 43.
14. Garvey, *Wonder*, 10.

ing to Garvey.[15] We "sit before the silence at the depth of everything made . . ."[16] By spending time alone, being silent and being still, we enter into the silence that can be heard in between the words.

While reading the text, a word other than the one presented may get the reader's attention. In this case, the reader should follow the guidance of the Spirit and use his or her word for the *Lectio Divina* process of reading, reflecting, journaling/meditating, and praying or contemplating.

3. **Reflection**: The Scripture passage is followed by a two-paragraph reflection on the biblical passage, its context, similar biblical material, and its possible application for the reader.

   Throughout the reflections, the masculine pronoun for God, LORD, LORD God, etc. is used. The author is well aware that God is neither male nor female, but in order to avoid the repetition of nouns over and over again, he employs male pronouns, as they are also used in most biblical translations.

4. **Journal/Meditation**: The reflection is followed by a question for journaling and/or personal meditation. The question functions as a guide for personal appropriation of silence, thus leading the reader into journaling and/or personal prayer. The journal/meditation question is designed to foster a process of actively applying the reflection to one's life and further development of it. The question gets one started; where the journal/meditation goes cannot be predetermined. It may be a single statement or an idea with which one lingers for a few minutes, a few hours, or a few days. Such contemplation has no end; the reader decides when he or she has finished his or her exploration because he or she needs to attend to other things. People who like to journal—written or electronic—will find the question appropriate for that activity.

   According to Scobey:

---

15. Ibid., 5.

16. Ibid., 10.

Meditation involves quieting the mind and heart. It is a time of focusing our attention on a sacred word or on our breath; a time of letting our thoughts pass by, without holding onto them or entering into them. It is a time of deep awareness. . . . A common theme . . . is silence and stillness. Contemplation, a cousin of meditation, was explained by St. Gregory the Great in the sixth century as "resting in God." St. Gregory went on to explain that in this "resting," the mind and heart are not so much seeking God as beginning to experience God's actual presence. The reduction of action and thought, according to St. Gregory, allows the person practicing contemplation to sustain [his or her] consent to God's presence. In other words—without action and thought, less gets in the way of experiencing God.[17]

In *Rosarium Virginis Mariae*, Pope St. John Paul II states, "Listening and mediation are nourished by silence."[18] He continues: "A discovery of the importance of silence is one of the secrets of practicing contemplation and mediation. One drawback of a society dominated by technology and the mass media is the fact that silence becomes increasingly difficult to achieve. . . . [I]t is fitting to pause briefly after listening to the word of God, while the mind focuses on the content" of the biblical passage and the reflection.[19]

"Just being comfortable with silence is being comfortable with allowing things to be just what they are, which is the basic practice of meditation," according to Mirabi Bush.[20] She adds, "Silence allows [one] to be receptive because [he or she is] not busy talking. Silence allows [a person] to listen deeply, and just be."[21]

---

17. Ibid., 43–44.

18. John Paul II, *Rosarium*, par. 31.

19. Ibid.

20. Petersen, "Working," 62.

21. Ibid.

5. **Prayer:** A prayer concludes the exercise and summarizes the original word in the title, which was illustrated by the Scripture, explored in the reflection, and served as the foundation for the journal/meditation exercise.

Through the sounds of sheer silence, the reader will develop a biblical spirituality that transforms him or her into a raised awareness of, a deeper knowledge of, and a closer relationship with the divine.

Mark G. Boyer

1 Silence

Primeval Silence

Scripture: ". . . [T]he world shall be turned back to primeval silence for seven days, as it was at the first beginnings, so that no one shall be left." (2 Esd 7:30)

Reflection: The apocalyptic section of OT (A) Second Esdras declares that just as it took seven days for God to create the world—technically six days of creation and one of rest (Gen 1:1–2:3)—so it will take seven days for its destruction to be completed and for it to return to primeval silence. Primeval silence is defined earlier in the book: ". . . [T]he spirit was blowing and darkness and silence embraced everything; the sound of human voices was not yet there" (2 Esd 6:39; cf. Gen 1:1–2). Thus, primeval silence is that absolute quiet that existed before God spoke light into existence. It is impossible to define primeval silence adequately, because the definition of silence is known basically from its opposite: noise. Thus, silence is the absence or lack of noise or human speech. According to the HB (OT) book of Genesis, God broke primeval silence by speaking his first word: light.

When the prophet Elijah flees to Mount Horeb (Sinai) to escape the wrath of Queen Jezebel of Israel, he experiences God in "a sound of sheer silence" (1 Kgs 19:12), which is much like the primeval silence heard only by God. "A sound of sheer silence" is an oxymoronic attempt to capture the idea of silence being the opposite of sound; a sound of complete and utter (the meaning of *sheer*) silence is the sound of no sound! The author of the OT (A) book of Wisdom (of Solomon) describes the tenth plague—the slaying of the firstborn—in Egypt as taking place "while gentle silence enveloped all things" (Wis 18:14). Echoing the opening lines of the HB (OT) book of Genesis, the author of the book of Wisdom declares that God's "all-powerful word leaped from heaven, from the royal throne" (Wis 18:15). The word leaping from heaven echoes God speaking the first word ever heard in the HB (OT) book of Genesis: "Let there be light" (Gen 1:3).

Journal/Meditation: Have you ever heard the sound of silence? How would you describe it? How did you recognize the divine presence?

Prayer: O LORD, your Spirit blows and darkness and silence embrace everything. Then, I can hear a sound of sheer silence and recognize your presence. Envelope me with your gentle silence now and forever. Amen.

Silence!

Scripture: ". . . [W]hen the Israelites cried out to the LORD, the LORD raised up for them a delivered, Ehud son of Gera, the Benjaminite, a left-handed man. The Israelites sent tribute by him to King Eglon of Moab. [Ehud said to King Eglon,] 'I have a secret message for you, O king.' So the king said, 'Silence!' and all his attendants went out from his presence." (Judg 3:15, 19)

Reflection: One of the lesser-known judge-liberators in the HB (OT) book of Judges is Ehud, distinguished by his being left-handed. In the ancient world, the right hand represents power, and the left hand represents powerlessness! However, after meeting alone with King Eglon of Moab, who has been the LORD's strength to punish the Israelites for eighteen years because of their doing evil (Judg 3:12–14), King Eglon thinks that Ehud is going to deliver a divine oracle to him. That is why he shouts, "Silence." Meanwhile, Ehud hides his sword on his right side, where King Eglon would not expect to see it. Ehud draws it with his so-thought powerless left hand and dispatches the king before escaping and giving rest to Israel from Moab for eighty years. Ehud's powerless left hand becomes more powerful than his right hand; with it he delivers his people from the oppression of Moab. Thus, Eglon's cry of "Silence!" is a double entendre; he calls for the very physical silence into which he is plunged by Ehud's sword.

Saying "Silence!" is a means of getting a group of people to be quiet. Shouting "Silence!" may bring people to the point where there is the lack of audible sound or the presence of sounds of very low intensity. In other words, there is an absence of communication or hearing, including any media other than speech and music. Eglon's cry for "Silence!" heralded his eternally-silent death. If thought about carefully, every call of "Silence!" requests the absence of sound which one day awaits every mortal being. The prophet Habakkuk illustrates the best time to shout "Silence!" He writes, "[T]he LORD is in his holy temple; silence before him, all the earth!" (Hab 2:20, NABRE)

Journal/Meditation: When do you shout "Silence!" to others or to yourself in recognition of the LORD's presence?

Prayer: In the midst of your creation, O God, I find myself in your holy temple. See me bowing before you in silent worship and bless me with your divine silence today, tomorrow, and forever. Amen.

Keep Silence

Scripture: "For everything there is a season, and a time for every matter under heaven: a time to keep silence . . . ." (Ecc 3:1, 7b)

Reflection: The author of the HB (OT) book of Ecclesiastes presents a poem contrasting extremes in the first eight verses of chapter 3. The interest here is only one of those extremes, namely, keeping silence. Moses emphasized keeping silence when he spoke to the Israelites, saying, "Keep silence and hear, O Israel! This very day you have become the people of the LORD, your God" (Deut 27:9). While reminiscing about his past, Job mentions his contemporaries who used to wait to listen to him "and kept silence for [his] counsel" (Job 29:21). Later, he acknowledges how he "kept silence, and did not go out of doors" (Job 31:34c). The prophet Habakkuk declares, ". . . [The LORD is in his holy temple; let all the earth keep silence before him!" (Hab 2:20)

Silence is often hard to find. While sitting at the computer, its fan makes a soft noise. The refrigerator runs. The air conditioner outside the window gentle roars as the furnace fan rotates in the utility room. The office chair squeaks. A passing car alerts attention. Someone is talking outside and down the street. The dog walks across the tile floor and her toe nails leave the sound of soft steps until she sits down. Silence trumps speaking; it just has to be found in a world of noise. Ecclesiasticus is correct: There is a time to keep silence in order to hear what God has to say. The challenge is to find the time and the silence.

Journal/Meditation: When have you kept silence and heard God speak to you?

Prayer: In your time-filled world, O LORD, there are occasions to keep silence, and there are occasions when I should speak. Fill me with the silence of the Holy Spirit and grant that I may one day enjoy timeless silence in your presence forever. Amen.

Not Keep Silence

Scripture: "For everything there is a season, and a time for every matter under heaven: a time to speak . . . ." (Ecc 3:1, 7b)

Reflection: The opposite of keeping silence is speaking. The author of the HB (OT) book of Ecclesiastes presents a poem contrasting extremes in the first eight verses of chapter 3. The interest here is only one of those extremes, namely, not keeping silence. This is the advice that Mordecai sends to his niece, Esther, queen-wife of King Ahasuerus of Susa, concerning the plot of Haman, the king's second in command, to eradicate the Jews: ". . . [I]f you keep silence at such a time as this, relief and deliverance will rise for the Jews from another quarter, but you and your father's family will perish" (Esth 4:14a). Similarly, when describing Leviathan, the ancient sea monster, God declares, "I will not keep silence concerning its limbs, or its mighty strength, or its splendid frame" (Job 41:12). In other words, there are times when one cannot keep silence.

One psalmist declares that God comes to Zion, the mountain upon which Jerusalem is built, in a theophany. "Our God comes and does not keep silence," sings the psalmist, "before him is a devouring fire, and a mighty tempest all around him" (Ps 50:3). Another psalmist addresses the LORD, declaring, "O God, do not keep silence; do not hold your peace or be still, O God!" (Ps 83:1) The song tells God all about the many enemies conspiring against his people and how God needs to act to save his people. "Let them know that you alone, whose name is the LORD, are the Most High over all the earth," concludes the psalmist (Ps 83:18). When enemies are surrounding a person, the time for keeping silence has ended. One cannot keep silence when any type of need arises.

Journal/Meditation: When have you found it necessary not to keep silence?

Prayer: O God, come and do not keep silence. Come in a devouring fire and in a mighty tempest. Do not hold your peace or be still, O LORD. Let all people know that you alone are the Most High over all the earth now and forever. Amen.

There was Silence

Scripture: "[The spirit] stood still, but I could not discern its appearance. A form was before my eyes; there was silence, then I heard a voice." (Job 4:16)

Reflection: Eliphaz the Temanite recounts a dream—"visions of the night" (Job 4:13)—in which he learns how insignificant human beings are. In deep sleep, he experiences trembling while hearing words, feeling a spirit pass his face, and watching goose bumps appear on his flesh (Job 4:12–15). Unable to discern the figure or appearance of the ghost, he saw a form and then "there was silence" (Job 4:16) and he heard the divine voice ask: "Can mortals be righteous before God? Can human beings be pure before their Maker?" (Job 4:17) The obvious answer to both questions is No! All one can do is seek God and commit one's cause to him (Job 5:8). He is in charge of all (Job 5:9–26). Psalm 65 further emphasizes this biblical point. The psalmist declares that only God silences the roaring of the seas, the roaring of their waves, and the tumult of the people of the earth (Ps 65:7).

The CB (NT) book of Revelation presents silence as primeval renewal: "When the Lamb opened the seventh seal, there was silence in heaven for about half an hour" (Rev. 8:1). Revelation's silence is also to prepare for the next event in the apocalyptic book, while it echoes the OT (A) book of Second Esdras' description of primeval silence. The Lord tells Esdras that his son, the Messiah, will be revealed, and for four hundred years people will rejoice. Then, the son will die, and the world will be turned back to primeval silence for seven days. After this, the earth will give up those who sleep in it and rest in it in silence. Then the Most High will enact judgment (2 Esd 7:26–34). In the book of Revelation, the silence prepares for incense smoke and trumpet blasts, both of which are elements of a theophany, namely, the manifestation of God. Silence precedes hearing the voice of God; silence is required to hear the Lord speak.

Journal/Meditation: What silence have you heard and known to be the presence of God?

Prayer: All praise is due to you, O God, who answer all prayer. Silence the roaring of seas and waves, of people and machines, of wind and leaves that I may hear your voice. Bestow the grace of righteousness upon me through your Son, the Messiah, Jesus Christ, who is Lord forever and ever. Amen.

Wait in Silence

Scripture: "For God alone my soul waits in silence; from him comes my salvation. For God alone my soul waits in silence, for my hope is from him." (Ps 62:1, 5)

Reflection: As the psalmist makes clear, human salvation and human hope are dependent upon God. In the biblical world, people thought that God was in charge of everything. That is why, as the psalmist sings, "He alone is my rock and my salvation, my fortress; I shall never be shaken" (Ps 65:2). All that insignificant human beings can do is wait in silence. After Zophar the Naamathite asks Job, "Should your babble put others to silence . . . ?" (Job 11:3), Job responds, "Let me have silence, and I will speak, and let come on me what may" (Job 13:13). Job waited in silence for Zophar to finish his presentation so that he could, in turn, call for silence to be heard.

The words of the psalmist are put into action by the eldest of Abraham's servants when he sends him to Nahor, Abraham's brother, to find a wife for Isaac, Abraham's son (Gen 24:1–14). After he arrives, he notices Rebekah (Abraham's great niece), daughter of Bethuel, Nahor's son (Abraham's nephew). According to Genesis, "The man gazed at her in silence to learn whether or not the LORD had made his journey successful" (Gen 24:21). In other words, he waited for God in silence. The Genesis story continues by narrating the servant's dealings with Rebekah's family and her going with him to marry Isaac (Gen 24:22–67). Throughout the narrative, the servant repeats that God makes journeys successful for those who wait in silence for him to act.

Journal/Meditation: When have you waited in silence for God to act? Was your journey successful?

Prayer: Blessed be the LORD, the God of Abraham, who does not forsake his steadfast love and his faithfulness toward people who wait in silence for his salvation. Strengthen my hope, O God, for in you alone my soul waits in silence today, tomorrow, and forever. Amen.

Kept Silence

Scripture: "The whole assembly kept silence, and listened to Barnabas and Paul as they told of all the signs and wonders that God had done through them among the Gentiles." (Acts 15:12)

Reflection: The first time the apostles had to gather in order to solve a problem was narrated by the author of the Acts of the Apostles—the same author who wrote Luke's Gospel—in chapter 15. There were some among the early movement—that later became known as Christianity—who taught that it was necessary for the Gentiles to become Jews before becoming Christian. This meant circumcision (Acts 15:1). As a result of the debate about this between certain unnamed individuals from Judea and Paul and Barnabas, the question was brought to the apostles in Jerusalem (Acts 15:2–11). As part of the discussion, Paul and Barnabas, who is featured as Paul's missionary companion throughout most of the Acts (4:36; 9:27; 11:22, 25, 30; 12:25; 13:1–2, 7, 42–43, 46, 52; 14:1, 12, 14, 20; 15:2, 12, 22, 25, 35–37, 39), told the whole assembly, which kept silence, about the divine signs and wonders they had witnessed. The members of the assembly—apostles and elders—kept silence in order to hear the words of Paul and Barnabas as they interpreted what God was doing through them. All kept silence in order to discern how to answer the question. Ultimately, it was decided that Gentiles did not have to become Jews before becoming Christians (Acts 15:2–35).

The psalmist sings about how he kept silence: "While I kept silence, my body wasted away through my groaning all day long" (Ps 32:3). The silence kept by the psalmist is an attempt to hide his unnamed sin, which causes him to groan all day while he does not eat. Once he breaks his silence and confesses his sin to the LORD, he discovers that God forgives him (Ps 32:1–2). He also declares that God's steadfast love surrounds those who trust in God (Ps 32:10). They are glad, rejoice, and shout for joy (Ps 32:11). The message of the psalmist is simple: There is no reason to keep silence about sin, that is, hide one's iniquity; the LORD forgives transgressions and removes the guilt of sin (Ps 32:5) for both Jews and Gentiles.

Journal/Meditation: What were the effects when you kept silence instead of confessing your sin?

Prayer: O LORD, all who are faithful offer prayer to you. At times of distress you rescue those who confess their transgressions to you. Grant that your steadfast love may be my hiding place where you protect me, O LORD, now and forever. Amen.

Learn in Silence

Scripture: ". . . [I]t is God's will that by doing right you should silence the ignorance of the foolish." (1 Pet 2:15)

Reflection: The end-of-the-first-century letter, known as First Peter, written by an unknown author in the name of the apostle Peter, urges his readers to accept secular authority for the Lord's sake (1 Pet 2:13–14). By doing so, that is, engaging in correct behavior, believers silence the ignorance of the foolish. Peter is functioning as a teacher here, instructing his students to learn in silence what is right and to do it. Solid learning put into action silences the ignorance of the foolish. Likewise, adherence to secular authority will serve as good example to non-believers. Good citizenship, according to First Peter, is God's will.

In the Letter to Titus, the second-generation Pauline author identifies rebellious people, idle talkers, and deceivers as those advocating circumcision (Titus 1:10). He writes, "They must be silenced, since they are upsetting whole families by teaching for sordid gain what it is not right to teach" (Titus 1:11). Those who insist that Gentiles be circumcised upset members of the Christian community for years; that is why Titus is told to silence them. Learning in silence is one of the topics of the First Letter to Timothy, written by a second-generation Pauline follower. Indicating a return to a patriarchal culture, the author states, "Let a woman learn in silence with full submission" (1 Tim 2:11). This could not have been written by authentic Paul, since he mentions many women who pastor churches (Rom 16:1–4, 6–7, 12; 1 Cor 16:19). The basic idea of learning in silence, applied to both men and women, is that there certainly is a time to learn in silence. When sinking into ignorance or when teaching falsehoods, silence can foster learning.

Journal/Meditation: What has been your most recent experience of learning in silence? Explain.

Prayer: During primeval silence, you spoke, LORD God, and everything came to be that had not yet existed. Fill me with your Spirit of Wisdom that out of silence I will have the right words to speak to ignorance and so praise you, eternal Trinity—Father, Son, and Holy Spirit—forever and ever. Amen.

Sit in Silence

Scripture: "Sit in silence, and go into darkness, daughter Chaldea! For you shall no more be called the mistress of kingdoms." (Isa 47:5)

Reflection: The prophet Isaiah describes the fall of Babylon (Chaldea) to King Cyrus of Persia. Babylon had conquered many nations—including Judah—and plundered and humiliated them. In the poem in Isaiah 47, the prophet writes harsh words about Babylon. His fifteen verses of poetic text describe Babylon, the once-upon-a-time world power, as sitting in silence and darkness. Those words are similar to how the author of the HB (OT) book of Lamentations describes the destruction of Jerusalem by Babylon at a previous time. "The elders of daughter Zion sit on the ground in silence" (Lam 2:10); later the author adds that it is good for one "to sit alone in silence when the Lord has imposed it" (Lam 3:28). Biblically, one can also sit in silence in the land of silence. Sheol, otherwise known as the underworld or netherworld, is the first level of a three-storied universe (the second story is the earth, and the third story is the heaven). The author of Psalm 94 declares, "If the LORD had not been my help, my soul would soon have lived in the land of silence" (Ps 94:17). The OT (A) book of Second Esdras describes the final judgment, stating, "The earth shall give up those who are asleep in it, and the dust those who rest there in silence" (2 Esd 7:32a). Psalm 115 is more explicit, stating,

"The dead do not praise the LORD, nor do any that go down into silence" (Ps 115:17). Thus, essentially, the duty of the living is to bless and praise God.

It is hard to sit alone in silence because it seems to envelop one like darkness. It is like going deep into a small cave, the underworld, the land of silence. God, however, is in the darkness and the silence, just like God is in the light and the voices. God can be found on every level of the three-storied universe. Thus, sitting alone in silence can be imposed by God, even if the person sitting presumes to impose it upon himself or herself. Taking a journey into the silence of the alone self to discover one's true self and, simultaneously, one's false self, is a great spiritual exercise.

Journal/Meditation: When have you last sat in silence? How would you describe it? What did you learn about God? about yourself?

Prayer: O LORD, you have been mindful of me, and you have blessed me. Envelop me in the silence of your steadfast love, and I will bless you from this time on and forevermore. Amen.

Motion for Silence

Scripture: "When [the tribune] had given him permission to speak, Paul stood on the steps and motioned to the people for silence; and when there was a great hush, he addressed them in the Hebrew language . . . ." (Acts 21:40)

Reflection: The author of the CB (NT) Acts of the Apostles— the same person who wrote Luke's Gospel—likes to use the line about motioning for silence, as presented in Acts 21:40. He used it before describing a certain Alexander, who "motioned for silence" (Acts 19:33). Earlier, he had written about Paul, who stood up "and with a gesture began to speak" (Acts 13:16a), and later again about Paul, who "stretched out his hand and began to defend himself" (Acts 26:26b). This motion for silence with the hand is a rhetorical gesture for an orator to initiate silence and attention. Older biblical translations often refer to the gesture as beckoning with one's hand or beckoning for silence.

Today, its equivalent might be a long and loud Shhh! with one's forefinger placed horizontally across one's lips. Another equivalent might be the person who approaches a podium, flicks the microphone with his or her finger, and asks, "Is this on?" A third form of getting silence consists in someone taking a microphone and saying, "Attention! Please take your seats; we are ready to begin." A person may look at another and say, "Hush!" And the silence follows the hush as it is passed on to others. However, the most effective method of initiating silence is to get a few people to be silent—maybe with the Shhh! or Hush! and a finger over the lips—and to let the action pass on to others until everyone is silent.

Journal/Meditation: What action do you use to bring about silence in a group?

Prayer: Heavenly Father, you broke the ancient silence when you spoke your first words of creation. Now, your wonderful universe brings me to a quiet hush as I see all that you have made. One day bring me to the eternal silence of your kingdom, where Jesus is Lord forever and ever. Amen.

Miscellaneous Silence

Scripture: "Listen to me in silence, O coastlands." (Isa 41:1a)

Reflection: The Bible contains a number of reflections on silence. For example, there are Isaiah's words addressed to the coastlands to listen in silence. Coastlands, the most distant parts of the earth, have no ears; therefore, this metaphor limps until the reader discovers that these are God's words echoing all across the world. The "I am your God" indicates that someone divine is at work here (Isa 41:10). Likewise, Jeremiah's words to Moab, one of Israel's bitter enemies, declare that the country "shall be brought to silence" (Jer 48:2d). Ezekiel records the Lord GOD's words to Tyre: "I will silence the music of your songs" (Ezek 26:13). In a similar vein the psalmist sings about how the LORD silences the enemy and the avenger through the mouths of babes and infants (Ps 8:2). Put plainly and simply: People should listen to God in silence.

The first letter of Ptolemy, recorded in the OT (A) book of Third Maccabees, narrates how Ptolemy IV Philopator, king of Egypt (221–204 BCE), offered citizenship to the Jews in Alexandria who, according to Ptolemy's letter, "both by speech and by silence . . . abominate[d] those few among them who [were] sincerely disposed toward [him]" (3 Macc 3:23). In other words, some Jews thought they were giving good example to fellow Jews by fostering silence to reject Ptolemy's offer of Egyptian citizenship. They probably had not read the words of the OT (A) book of Sirach: "Be ashamed . . . of silence, before those who greet you" (Sir 41:19b–20a). Thus, both books do not foster silence, but they do not do so for different reasons. The Bible contains God's words advocating silence and the same God's words not advocating it. It remains the decision of the individual person to listen in silence or to break the silence with words.

Journal/Meditation: Identify situations when you keep silence and when you do not. In general, is there a theme that ties together your keeping silence times? Is there a theme that ties together your not keeping silence times?

Prayer: LORD, you are first, and you will be last. Open my ears to hear you speaking to me in silence. With your Holy Spirit renew me and strengthen me as a follower of your Son, Jesus Christ, who lives and reigns forever and ever. Amen.

2

Silent

Be Silent! 1

Scripture: "Be silent!" (Amos 8:3b)

Reflection: The two-word exclamation of the Lord GOD to the prophet Amos is a command for him to shut up and not respond to the words he has just heard about the coming judgment of Israel (Amos 8:1–3). God, who is not silent to his people (Ps 28:1b), wants Amos to listen attentively. In telling his prophet to hush, God silences him and exercises authority over him. The author of Mark's Gospel portrays Jesus saying the same words in order to exercise authority over a man with an unclean spirit. Jesus says, "Be silent, and come out of him" (Mark 1:25; cf. Luke 4:35). In Luke's Gospel, the angel Gabriel, who stands in the presence of God (Luke 1:19), silences Zechariah, telling him that he will become mute, unable to speak, until the day when John the Baptist is born to him and his wife, Elizabeth, in their older years (Luke 1:20).

In his First Letter to the Corinthians, Paul states that if there is no one to interpret what those speaking in tongues are saying, "[L]et them be silent in church and speak to themselves and to

God" (1 Cor 14:28). Likewise, the community is directed to let two or three prophets speak, but "[i]f a revelation is made to someone else sitting nearby, let the first person be silent" (1 Cor 14:30). Silence trumps the speaking in tongues and a prophetic utterance! At a later time, someone inserted the line that "women should be silent in the churches" (1 Cor 14:34) into First Corinthians, but this is a later addition by someone—other than Paul—who was attempting to restore patriarchy; it contradicts 1 Corinthians 11:2–16. What all these be-silent biblical passages have in common is this: Telling another to be silent exercises authority over him or her for some reason. Good advice about being silent is sung by the psalmist: "When you are disturbed, do not sin; ponder it on your beds, and be silent" (Ps 4:4). While people can be silent, God cannot be silent.

Journal/Meditation: Who has exercised authority over you by telling you, "Be silent!"?

Prayer: To you, O LORD, I call. In your mercy, do not refuse to hear me. If you are silent, I shall be like those who enter the netherworld. Hear my voice of supplication, and see my hands lifted up to you, who are God forever and ever. Amen.

Be Silent! 2

Scripture: "Be silent, all people, before the LORD; for he has roused himself from his holy dwelling." (Zech 2:13)

Reflection: The prophet Zechariah's words to be silent before the LORD are echoed by the prophet Zephaniah's words: "Be silent before the Lord GOD! For the day of the LORD is at hand" (Zeph 1:7a). To be silent before God—either because he has roused himself or his day is at hand—is a stance advocated often in biblical literature. Why? Because it is the only posture a human being, created by God, can take when being in the presence of the all-powerful Creator. In the words of Isaiah, people are the clay, and the LORD is the potter; this makes all the work of God's hands (Isa 64:8). And the only stance clay can take before the Potter is silence.

The theme of silence is also found in the HB (OT) book of Job. Job responds to Eliphaz's first speech, saying, "Teach me, and I will be silent; make me understand how I have gone wrong" (Job 6:24). In his response to Zophar, Job expresses his desire to bring his case of unjust suffering before God, asking, "Who is there that will contend with me? For then I would be silent and die" (Job 13:19). About three-quarters of the way through the book, Elihu says to Job, "Pay heed, Job, listen to me; be silent, and I will speak. If you have anything to say, answer me; speak, for I desire to justify you. If not, listen to me; be silent, and I will teach you wisdom" (Job 33:31–33). Similarly, the prophet Elisha responds to the words of the company of prophets—who tell him, "Do you know that today the LORD will take your master away from you?"—saying, "Yes, I know; be silent" (2 Kgs 2:5). Be silent before God. Be silent before those prophets who speak for God and learn wisdom or watch God perform a marvelous deed, like taking Elijah to heaven in a whirlwind (2 Kgs 2:11).

Journal/Meditation: When have you been silent before the all-power Creator? What did you hear?

Prayer: I am silent before you, Lord GOD. Rouse yourself from your heavenly dwelling and hear my prayer. Make me ready for the fullness of your kingdom, where you live and reign as a Trinity of Father, Son, and Holy Spirit, one God, forever and ever Amen.

Not Be Silent

Scripture: "One night the Lord said to Paul in a vision, 'Do not be afraid, but speak and do not be silent; for I am with you, and no one will lay a hand on you to harm you, for there are many in this city who are my people.'" (Acts 18:9–10)

Reflection: Just as there are times to be silent, there are also times not to be silent. This is illustrated by the author of the Acts of the Apostles when he narrates a story about a vision Paul had in Corinth. While there are other elements of visions, the primary one used in Paul's is the voice of the Lord Jesus, which is similar to the voice Paul heard on his way to Damascus (Acts 9:4–6). Jesus tells Paul not to be afraid, another element of visions, but to speak and not to be silent. Then, Jesus assures the apostle that he is with him to protect him from all harm, another element of visions (Isa 41:10, 43:5; Jer 1:8, 19; Matt 28:20). In a similar vein, Ezra narrates his restoration of the Scriptures. He hears a voice telling him to drink a fire-colored liquid, which opens his mouth to dictate the texts. "I spoke in the daytime and was not silent at night," he writes (2 Esd 14:43).

The psalms are filled with pleas to God not to be silent. Within the twenty-eight verses of Psalm 35, a prayer for help against enemies, the singer addresses the LORD, saying, "You have seen, O LORD; do not be silent! O LORD, do not be far from me! Wake up! Bestir yourself for my defense, for my cause, my God and my Lord! (Ps 35:22–23) Similarly, Psalm 109 begins, "Do not be silent, O God of my praise" (Ps 109:1). Psalm 30 begins by praising the LORD for having helped the petitioner "so that [his] soul may praise him and not be silent" (Ps 30:12a). If God is silent, the wicked may triumph. However, the LORD hears and saves those who call upon him.

Journal/Meditation: When have you asked God not to be silent? What response did you get?

Prayer: O LORD, my God, you see the actions of all people. Do not be silent to my prayer for the help of the Holy Spirit. Remove my fear and give me the words to speak about your Son, Jesus Christ, who lives and reigns forever and ever. Amen.

Keep Silent! 1

Scripture: "Even fools who keep silent are considered wise; when they close their lips, they are deemed intelligent." (Prov 17:28)

Reflection: According to the HB (OT) book of Proverbs, keeping silent may indicate a person's intelligence. According to proverbial wisdom literature, fools who keep silent are often considered to be wise. This sentiment is echoed by Job's words to his friends, "If you would only keep silent, that would be your wisdom!" (Job 13:5) There is a stinging quality to Job's words! The prophet Amos adds to the wisdom of keeping silent, stating, ". . . [T]he prudent will keep silent in such a time [of judicial and economic abuse]; for it is an evil time" (Amos 5:13). Thus, according to biblical literature there is a type of wise silence which indicates intelligence. This idea, of course, contradicts the usual human presupposition that more talking will solve the problem.

In chapter 64, the prophet Isaiah records a plea to God to tear open the heavens and to come down to the earth and help solve the conflicts associated with the rebuilding of the Temple between 520 and 516 BCE. According to Isaiah, the then-present situation seemed to be a contradiction of God's power. He is the potter, and his people are the clay waiting to be shaped (Isa 64:8). The desolation of Jerusalem and the Temple were caused by the Babylonians in 587 BCE, and the people who returned to Jerusalem were not organized enough to get busy rebuilding. "After all this," asks Isaiah, "will you restrain yourself, O LORD? Will you keep silent, and punish us so severely?" (Isa 64:12) Later, the Jews realize that God is exercising wise silence. As Isaiah records, they begin to realize that the LORD is interested in the humble and contrite in spirit, those who tremble at his word, more than he cares about a rebuilt Temple (Isa 66:2). And with that insight, they are on the path to wise silence.

Journal/Meditation: When have you recently practiced wise silence which displayed your intelligence?

Prayer: All-wise God, before you spoke the first word ever heard, you dwelt in silence. With the aid of the Holy Spirit make me wise in silence that I may contemplate your wonderful works through Jesus Christ, your Son, who is Lord forever and ever. Amen.

Keep Silent! 2

Scripture: "The company of prophets who were in Bethel came out to Elisha, and said to him, 'Do you know that today the LORD will take your master away from you?' And he said, 'Yes, I know; keep silent.'" (2 Kgs 2:3)

Reflection: There are occasions in life when the right thing to do is to keep silent. The company of prophets—followers of prophets—tells Elisha, soon-to-be-successor to Elijah, that Elijah will be taken away. Elisha, who is already aware that Elijah's ascension into heaven in a whirlwind (2 Kgs 2:11) is about to occur, merely tells them to keep silent before the awe-filled event about to take place. The fiery chariot and fiery horses which carry Elijah from earth to heaven is God in theophany.

Biblical literature mentions others who keep silent. For example, Peter, John, and James witness the appearance of Moses and Elijah to Jesus, while he is transfigured (Luke 9:28–36a). After witnessing this event, "they kept silent and in those days told no one any of the things they had seen" (Luke 9:36b). The author of Luke's Gospel, who is also the author of the Acts of the Apostles, records that once the apostles and elders met in Jerusalem to look into the question about the circumcision of the Gentiles, "[t]he whole assembly kept silence, and listened to Barnabas and Paul as they told of all the signs and wonders that God had done through them among the Gentiles" (Acts 15:12). Thus, there are occasions when it is best just to keep silent in order to recognize that God is revealing himself present in the world.

Journal/Meditation: What recent experience of keeping silent has brought you a deeper awareness of the divine presence?

Prayer: Father of Jesus, when people recognize your presence, they keep silent. Raise my awareness to hear your voice and acknowledge your signs and wonders this day. You are one God—Father, Son, and Holy Spirit—forever and ever. Amen.

Not Keep Silent

Scripture: "My anguish, my anguish! I writhe in pain! Oh, the walls of my heart! My heart is beating wildly; I cannot keep silent; for I hear the sound of the trumpet, the alarm of war." (Jer 4:19)

Reflection: It is impossible to keep silent at times. Even God cannot keep silent, as illustrated by the prophet Jeremiah. The LORD speaks in judgment against Judah and Jerusalem and brings the enemy to punish his people. But, as recorded by Jeremiah, God is in anguish as he watches the battle; he twists and rolls in pain. His heart aches because it is beating wildly within his chest. He cannot keep silent even though he hears the enemy's trumpet blasts signaling that war is beginning. Jeremiah's words about the LORD's huge, breaking heart are similar to verses found in the prophet Isaiah. "For Zion's sake I will not keep silent, and for Jerusalem's sake I will not rest, until her vindication shines out like the dawn, and her salvation like a burning torch," says God (Isa 62:1). Again, the LORD declares, "I will not keep silent, but I will repay" (Isa 65:6a).

If God cannot keep silent, then neither can people keep silent. When faced with an important moral decision concerning life and death, people cannot keep silent. When a decision involves one's family, one member cannot assume responsibility and keep silent. Likewise, one member of a family in anguish with terminal cancer cannot keep silent; giving others the opportunity to participate in the last days of a member's life is a gift. When too much is at stake for oneself and others, silence cannot be kept. Even God cannot keep silent; he is in anguish as he watches the destruction of the nation he called into existence.

Journal/Meditation: When did you not keep silent? Why did you choose to speak?

Prayer: Send your Holy Spirit to me, Father, that he may stir a remembrance of you in me. Then, I will not keep silent. I will proclaim your steadfast love and mercy. I will announce that you are one God—Father, Son, and Holy Spirit—forever and ever. Amen.

Silent Like Sheep

Scripture: "[My servant] was oppressed, and he was afflicted, yet he did not open his mouth; like a lamb that is led to the slaughter, or like a sheep that before its shearers is silent, so he did not open his mouth." (Isa 53:7)

Reflection: In the last of four servant passages found in the HB (OT) book of the prophet Isaiah, he describes the fate of Israel as the servant of God. In particular, the last passage focuses on the servant's suffering. His silence during his suffering is compared to that of a lamb about to be slaughtered and a sheep standing before its shearers. When the servant's suffering is about to be crowned with death, he remains silent like a lamb. When the servant's intense suffering is about to come to an end, he remains silent like a sheep before the shearers.

In a unique story found in the Acts of the Apostles, the above passage from Isaiah is being read by an Ethiopian eunuch, who was on his way home from Jerusalem after worshiping in the Temple there. Philip is sent by an angel of the Lord to the man in his chariot who was reading, "Like a sheep he was led to the slaughter, and like a lamb silent before its shearer, so he does not open his mouth" (Acts 8:32). "The eunuch asked Philip, 'About whom . . . does the prophet say this, about himself or about someone else?' Then Philip began to speak, and starting with this scripture, he proclaimed to him the good news about Jesus" (Acts 8:34–35). Philip takes the servant passage from Isaiah and proceeds to announce its fulfillment in Jesus, who was crucified. The author of John's Gospel takes the passage to an even higher level, declaring that Jesus is the lamb of God (John 1:29, 36) who dies at the same time as the Passover lambs are being slaughtered in the Temple (John 19:14). And the book of Revelation presents a vision of "a Lamb standing as if it had been slaughtered" (Rev 5:6).

Journal/Meditation: When have you been silent like a sheep in the face of suffering?

Prayer: Father of Jesus, when your Son was afflicted, he did not open his mouth. Like a lamb led to the slaughter, he was escorted to crucifixion. Like a sheep silent before its shearers, he did not condemn his persecutors. Shape me into the image of Jesus, who is Lord forever and ever. Amen.

Are Silent

Scripture: "When I am silent [rulers] will wait for me, and when I speak they will give heed; if I speak at greater length, they will put their hands on their mouths." (Wis 8:12)

Reflection: The OT (A) book of Wisdom, also known as the Wisdom of Solomon, is attributed to King Solomon of all Israel, even though it was written many years after his life. Nevertheless, Solomon is known for the wisdom God gave him (1 Kgs 3:10–14), and attributing a book to him adds credibility to the teaching found within it. In his reflection on his pursuit of understanding, he personifies wisdom as a woman whom he sought. Because he found her, she gave him glory among people, honor among the elders, and admiration by rulers (Wis 8:10–11). Thus, when Solomon is silent, the rulers will wait for him to speak; and, when he finally does speak for a long time, they put their hands over their mouths so as not to speak and to evoke silence.

Four leprous men find themselves left outside of the gate during the siege of Samaria by the Arameans. After little debate they decide to go to the Aramean camp in the hope of finding food. However, upon entering the camp, they find no one there; the enemy has fled. They enter two enemy tents and find food and other booty, some of which they carry off and hide (2 Kgs 7:3–8). Finally, the lepers say to one another, "What we are doing is wrong. This is a day of good news; if we are silent and wait until the morning light, we will be found guilty; therefore let us go and tell the king's household" (2 Kgs 7:9). It takes some doing for the king to hear the good news that his enemy has fled and left behind all the food he and his people need to alleviate the famine caused by the siege (2 Kgs 7:10–20). The lepers are like Solomon, displaying wisdom not only to themselves, but also to the ruler, the king.

Journal/Meditation: Have you ever had anyone be silent while waiting to hear words of wisdom from you? Explain.

Prayer: O LORD, O Rock, you cannot look on wrongdoing nor can you be silent when the wicked swallow the righteous. Give me the understanding of Solomon that I may announce the truth of the good news of Jesus Christ, your Son, who is wisdom now and forever. Amen.

Was Silent

Scripture: "I was silent and still; I held my peace to no avail; my distress grew worse. I am silent; I do not open my mouth, for it is you [, O Lord,] who have done it." (Ps 39:2, 9).

Reflection: The singer of Psalm 39 begins his prayer by recounting his vow to guard his ways so as not to sin with his tongue. "I will keep a muzzle on my mouth as long as the wicked are in my presence," he sings (Ps 39:1b). However, after narrating how he was silent and still (Ps 39:2), he begins to reflect on the transience of life; he sings about life being short and how a lifetime is nothing in the LORD's sight (Ps 39:4–5). Indeed, when compared to God, a human life is about a breath long. Ultimately, the psalmist discovers all that really matters is hope (Ps 39:7). In the face of such a realization, he is silent once again and does not open his mouth (Ps 39:9).

On some occasions the best stance to take is to be silent. Especially when a question has been posed, being silent enables the seeker to think about the deeper truth of the question. As the psalmist expresses, being silent opens people to God and his compassion, truth, and hope. This kind of deep truth takes time to understand. This type of being silent is illustrated by Moses' brother, Aaron. After Aaron's sons offer unholy fire to the LORD, they die (Lev 10:1–2). Moses explains to Aaron why this happened (Lev 10:3a). "And Aaron was silent" (Lev 10:3b). Jesus, too, demonstrates the power of being silent. When the high priest questions Jesus about why he does not answer his accusers (Mark 14:60), the narrator states, ". . . [H]e was silent and did not answer" (Mark 14:61a). The author of Matthew's Gospel shortens the narrative by writing, ". . . Jesus was silent." (Matt 26:63a). On some occasions being silent speaks a truth that cannot be heard in words.

Journal/Meditation: When have you remained silent, not opening your mouth, in order to plumb the deeper truth? What was that truth you discovered?

Prayer: O LORD, you guard my ways, keeping me silent and still. Make me realize the measure of my days and how fleeting this life is. Fill me with hope that comes from the Holy Spirit. Hear my prayer, O LORD, and give ear to my cry through your Son, Jesus Christ, now and forever. Amen.

Were Silent

Scripture: ". . . [T]he people were silent and answered [the Rabshakeh] not a word, for the king's command was, 'Do not answer him.'" (2 Kgs 18:36)

Reflection: Besides individual persons being silent, there are also biblical accounts of groups of people being silent. Representing the king of Assyria, the Rabshakeh speaks to the people of Judah urging them to surrender. When he finishes, they remain silent (Isa 36:13–21). Nehemiah records his words to the nobles and officials of Jerusalem who were taking interest from their own people during a famine. When Nehemiah finished chastising them, "They were silent, and could not find a word to say" (Neh 5:8b). As in the case when an individual says more by being silent than by speaking words, so it is that groups learn more when, after listening to another, all members of the group are silent. Group silence is often encountered at places like the 9/11 memorial, the Vietnam wall memorial, or the World War II memorial.

The author of Mark's Gospel narrates a story about Jesus entering a synagogue, in which he encounters a man with a withered hand. Those in the synagogue watch Jesus to see if he will work, that is, heal the man on the sabbath and, thus, break the law that forbids work on the last day of the week. Jesus asks the assembly, "'Is it lawful to do good or to do harm on the sabbath, to save life or to kill?' But they were silent" (Mark 3:4). In the Lukan version of the same story, Jesus is on the way to a Pharisee's house to eat when a man with dropsy appears. Jesus asks the lawyers and Pharisees,

"'Is it lawful to cure people on the sabbath, or not?' But they were silent" (Luke 14:3–4a). Jesus' disciples are embarrassingly silent after arguing about which one of them is greatest (Mark 9:33–34). The scribes and chief priests become silent after Jesus teaches them to give what belongs to God to him and what belongs to Caesar to him (Luke 20:19–26). Sometimes while worshiping with a church full of people, the group becomes silent, or while listening to a symphony orchestra, the audience becomes silent.

Journal/Meditation: When have you found yourself in a group of people who were silent? What truth did you discover in the group silence?

Prayer: Heavenly Father, while some praise you with song, others praise you with silence. Fill me with the silence of the Holy Spirit, and hear my silent prayer today through Jesus Christ my Lord. Amen.

Wisely Silent

Scripture: "When [the circumcised believers] heard [Peter], they were silenced. And they praised God, saying, 'Then God has given even to the Gentiles the repentance that leads to life.'" (Acts 11:18)

Reflection: Peter has just finished rehearsing to the Jewish believers in Jerusalem his experience with Gentiles upon whom the Holy Spirit fell in Joppa. The Jewish believers had criticized Peter for associating with uncircumcised men (Acts 11:3); however, after hearing his narration about the events surrounding the baptism of the Gentiles they were silenced and awestruck that God had given repentance to the Gentiles. Peter, a Jewish believer, could not keep his mouth closed. In the words of God to Ezekiel, he had to speak "and no longer be silent" (Ezek 24:27a). Peter's words in Jerusalem echo his words in Joppa: "I truly understand that God shows no partiality, but in every nation anyone who fears him and does what is right is acceptable to him" (Acts 10:34–35). Thus, Peter, who has been wisely silent, has found the occasion to speak wisely. He is like the LORD's words recorded by Isaiah about the sentinels walking the walls of Jerusalem: "[T]hey shall never be silent" (Isa 62:6b).

Even God declares that there comes a time to end being wisely silent. After recounting the deeds of the wicked in Psalm 50:16–20, God states, "These things you have done and I have been silent; you thought that I was one just like yourself" (Ps 50:21ab). Likewise 2 Esdras records God stating, "I will be silent no longer concerning their ungodly acts that they impiously commit, neither will I tolerate their wicked practices" (2 Esd 15:8a). When wisdom is combined with silence, a person has time to reflect upon certain deeds, like God's election of the Gentiles. Once the truth is discovered, however, then wisdom prompts the silencing of silence. When people begin to think that God is just like they are, then they need to listen as God breaks his own silence and speaks the truth.

Journal/Meditation: When have you found yourself speaking truth after being wisely silent? What truth did you present?

Prayer: LORD God, you summon the earth from the rising of the sun to its setting, and you come without keeping silence in order to name righteousness and wickedness. Guide me with your Holy Spirit to be wisely silent that I may be counted among the righteous now and forever. Amen.

Remain Silent

Scripture: "Whoever belittles another lacks sense, but an intelligent person remains silent." (Prov 11:12)

Reflection: A person's IQ or intelligence quotient is a total score derived from several standardized tests designed to assess human intelligence. Scores from intelligence tests are estimates of intelligence; they are used for educational placement, assessment of intellectual disability, and evaluating job applicants. According to the HB (OT) book of Proverbs, the best way to determine an intelligent person is to observe how well he or she remains silent! In other words, intelligence can be measured with a silence meter, as it is in the house of Philip the evangelist (Acts 21:8). The people gathered there urge Paul not to go to Jerusalem because he will be handed over to the Gentiles (Acts 21:12). Paul, however, states that he is willing even to die in Jerusalem for the name of Jesus (Acts 21:13). The narrator says, "Since he would not be persuaded, we remained silent except to say, 'The Lord's will be done'" (Acts 21:14).

The prophet Isaiah records the LORD's critical words to those who have returned from Babylonian captivity to rebuild Jerusalem. Bitter divisions have emerged among the returned exiles. God declares, "Israel's sentinels are blind, they are all without knowledge; they are all silent dogs that cannot bark; dreaming, lying down, loving to slumber" (Isa 56:10). While not comparing Israel's sentinels to silent dogs, the prophet Habakkuk addresses the issue of false gods: "Alas for you who say to the wood, 'Wake up!' to silent stone, 'Rouse yourself!' Can it teach? See it is gold and silver plated, and there is no breath in it at all" (Hab 2:19). These latter two instances serve as a warning for those who remain silent. Thus, there is a type of remaining silent that illustrates one's intelligence, and there is a type of remaining silent that illustrates ignorance.

Journal/Meditation: Recently, when you have demonstrated your intelligence by remaining silent? When you have demonstrated your ignorance by remaining silent?

Prayer: All-holy God, send your Holy Spirit to fill me with silence that demonstrates my intelligence before you. You, Father, live and reign in holy silence with your Son, Jesus Christ, in the unity of the Holy Spirit, one God, forever and ever. Amen.

3

Quiet

Be Quiet! 1

Scripture: ". . . [T]he Levites stilled all the people, saying, 'Be quiet, for this day is holy; do not be grieved.'" (Neh 8:11)

Reflection: Once the Jewish exiles have returned from Babylon to Jerusalem and rebuilt the city's walls, the HB (OT) book of Nehemiah records the inhabitants calling for Ezra, the priest and scribe, to read the law of Moses to them (Neh 8:1–8). The Levites, whose responsibility it is to teach the people the meaning of the law, tell the assembly to be quiet on the holy day. Likewise, the prophet Isaiah tells King Ahaz of Judah, when Jerusalem is about to be attacked, "Take heed, be quiet, do not fear, and do not let your heart be faint . . ." (Isa 7:4). The prophet Jeremiah records a song of the sword, writing, "Ah, sword of the LORD! How long until you are quiet? Put yourself into your scabbard, rest and be still! How can it be quiet, when the LORD has given it an order?" (Jer 47:6) The Second Book of Samuel records Absalom telling his full sister, Tamar, who had been raped by her half brother, Amnon, "Be quiet for now, my sister; he is your brother; do not take this to heart" (2 Sam 13:20b).

The biblical exhortation to be quiet is equivalent to the modern shout of "Shut up!" As all these miscellaneous instructions indicate, there is the need for someone, preferably a leader, to call for quiet. There is the need for someone to take charge of a situation and command all in attendance to stop talking. The Levites serve this function by telling the Jews to be quiet on the day declared to be holy. Isaiah is the leader who commands the king to be quiet even though his capital city is surrounded by his enemy. Jeremiah depicts God as the enemy ordering an attack. And while sentiments would be entirely different today when confronting a half brother raping his half sister, Absalom attempts to calm Tamar; the right time for Amnon's punishment will come (2 Sam 13:23–39). Thus, the exhortation for quiet requires a leader, who can take charge of a situation.

Journal/Meditation: When have you accepted the role of leadership and told others to be quiet?

Prayer: LORD God, you dwell in absolute quiet as Father, Son, and Holy Spirit. Give me the guidance to know when to call others to be quiet at times that are holy. Grant this wisdom in the name of Jesus, who quietly lives and reigns with you in the unity of the Holy Spirit, one God, forever and ever. Amen.

Be Quiet! 2

Scripture: "Many [people] sternly ordered [Bartimaeus, son of Timaeus, a blind beggar] to be quiet, but he cried out even more loudly, 'Son of David, have mercy on me!'" (Mark 10:48)

Reflection: After getting to Jericho and leaving there, Jesus encounters the blind beggar known as Bartimaeus sitting by the roadside. Of course, Bartimaeus hears that all the commotion surrounds Jesus of Nazareth passing by. The blind beggar, shouts, "Jesus, Son of David, have mercy on me!" (Mark 10:47) Many of those with Jesus tell the blind man to be quiet, but he keeps shouting until Jesus hears him, calls him, and heals his blindness because of his faith. After he is healed, the blind man, who can now see, becomes a follower of Jesus (Mark 10:46–52). The author of Matthew's Gospel removes the proper name from this account, and as he is fond of doing, replaces one blind man with two blind men (Matt 20:29–30), whom the crowd sternly order to be quiet (Matt 20:31). The author of Luke's Gospel leaves his Markan source intact, but removes the name of the blind beggar (Luke 18:35–43) and explains, "Those who were in front sternly ordered [the nameless blind man] to be quiet; but he shouted even more loudly, 'Son of David, have mercy on me!'" (Luke18:39). As in Mark, Jesus restores the man's sight and he follows him, just as he does in Matthew and Luke.

What the people in the crowd attempt to do is to hush the blind beggar. They want him to stop interrupting the procession of Jesus and his disciples through Jericho. Sternly, they order the blind man to be quiet. But in the presence of Jesus the healer, the man cannot be quiet. The blind man—without seeing—identifies Jesus as the Son of David, who can give him what he cannot earn and does not deserve: his sight. In Mark's Gospel, the crowd's words to the blind man to be quiet echo the words of others (usually demons) who know who Jesus is. Unknowingly, the author of Matthew's Gospel and Luke's Gospel copy this motif from Mark into their narratives. Jesus, as he does elsewhere, identifies faith in one presumed not to have it. And that blind man's faith is so strong that after he is healed of his blindness he is one of only a few who follow Jesus. The motif of secrecy as to the identify of Jesus throughout Mark's Gospel (except for the demons who always know who he is) is enacted by the crowd when the members tell the blind man to be quiet. The supreme irony is that the blind man sees and the seeing remain blind!

Journal/Meditation: When have you tried to hush someone only to discover the truth that he or she was speaking (to you)?

Prayer: Jesus, Son of David, have mercy on me. Remove the blindness of my eyes and my ears that in the quiet I may recognize you as the Son of the Father, who with you and the Holy Spirit are one God forever and ever. Amen.

Be Quiet! 3

Scripture: "Thus says the Lord to Ezra: 'Pause and be quiet, my people, because your rest will come.'" (2 Esd 2:10, 24)

Reflection: The words spoken by God to Ezra in the OT (A) book of Second Esdras promise the readers first place in his resurrection if the people but pause and be quiet (2 Esd 2:23–24). Ezra practices the words he writes from God after his own son dies on his wedding night (2 Esd 10:1). He writes, "I remained quiet until the evening of the second day. But when all of [my neighbors] had stopped consoling me, encouraging me to be quiet, I got up in the night and fled . . ." (2 Esd 10:2–3). Ezra goes to a field to mourn and fast (2 Esd 10:4). This type of being quiet is equivalent to trust. The Lord's words about pausing—stopping to reflect deeply upon the circumstances of a situation—and being quiet give people time to digest what is occurring and (re)discover their trust that God has everything under control. Most often this is needed at the time of death of a loved one, as demonstrated by Ezra at the death of his son. Pausing and being quiet calm the emotions of separation and, thus, enable the person to rest in trust of God.

Similarly, in the OT (A) book of Tobit, when Tobias fails to return to his parents, Tobit and Anna, Tobias's mother, thinks that he is dead and begins to mourn (Tob 10:1–5). "But Tobit kept saying to her, 'Be quiet and stop worrying, my dear, he is all right.' She answered him, 'Be quiet yourself! Stop trying to deceive me! My child has perished'" (Tob 10:6a, 7abc). Of course, the reader knows that Tobit's exhortation to Anna to be quiet and to trust is based on the fact that Tobias has been detained from his return home because he has married Sarah. Shortly, Tobias and Sarah will return to Tobit and Anna, and Tobit's words about pausing, being quiet, and trusting will be proved true.

Journal/Meditation: Recently, when have you paused, been quiet, and trusted God? Explain.

Prayer: Blessed be you, O God, and blessed be your great name. Grant me days to pause and to be quiet that I may recognize your Spirit at work in my life and in the lives of all I meet. At the end of my days, grant me rest with you, Father, with your Son, and with the Holy Spirit forever. Amen.

Keep Quiet

Scripture: "When the [Danite] men [, who were spies,] went into Micah's house and took the idol of cast metal, the ephod, and the teraphim, the priest [, Jonathan,] said to them, 'What are you doing?' They said to him, 'Keep quiet! Put your hand over your mouth, and come with us, and be to us a father and a priest.'" (Judg 18:18–19ab)

Reflection: The account in the HB (OT) book of Judges about the clan of the Danites searching for a home (Judg 17:1—18:31) explains how the city of Dan became a national shrine in the northern kingdom of Israel even though the true house of God was at Shiloh (1 Sam 1–2). A man named Micah employs a silversmith to create an idol, which he places in a shrine in his house. He also has an ephod, a priestly garment, and teraphim, figurines used to divine God's will. Micah then hires a Levite, named Jonathan, from Bethlehem in Judah, to be his household priest in the hope of the LORD prospering him (Judg 17:13). Jonathan and the idol, the ephod, and the teraphim are taken by the Danites to Dan, where they remain in a shrine "until the time the land went into captivity" (Judg 18:31) under the Assyrians. In order to take all Micah's household shrine's contents, the Danite spies order Jonathan to keep quiet by putting his hand over his mouth to insure a period of silence.

Often in Catholic elementary schools of the mid-twentieth century, nuns often quieted their talkative students by instructing them to put their hands over their mouths. This action insured quiet by all but the most creative of students. Similarly, the Gazites lay in wait and "kept quiet all night" (Judg 16:2c) in the hope of capturing Samson. Likewise, the priest Alcimus, after presenting gifts to King Demetrius, kept quiet during the day (2 Macc 14:3–4) in the hope of gaining the high priesthood through his treachery. In his suffering, Job curses the day of his birth by wishing that he was stillborn. "Now I would be lying down and quiet," he says; "I would be asleep; then I would be at rest" (Job 3:13). Later, Job's friend, Elihu, reflects on God, asking, "When he is quiet, who can condemn?" (Job 34:29a), while Psalm 107 praises the LORD, who rescues those in a storm on the sea in ships, who "were glad because they had quiet" (Ps 107:30a). Thus, the Bible presents reasons to be quiet: to steal a household god and its priest, to trap someone, to gain a position, to die at birth, or to experience a calm sea.

Journal/Meditation: What are your reasons to be quiet? Make a list for yourself.

Prayer: I give thanks to you, O LORD, for you are good, and your steadfast love endures forever. When the stormy winds of life lift up the waves of the sea, hear my prayer. Make the storm be still, hush the waves of the sea, and give me quiet through Jesus Christ my Lord. Amen.

Quiet and Peace

Scripture: ". . . [H]ave no fear, my servant Jacob, says the LORD, and do not be dismayed, O Israel; for I am going to save you from far away, and your offspring from the land of their captivity. Jacob shall return and have quiet and ease, and no one shall make him afraid." (Jer 30:10; 46:27)

Reflection: The prophet Jeremiah's words to the Jewish exiles in Babylon replace their terror with hope that they will return to Judah, where they will rediscover quiet and peace. Jeremiah's words echo David's narration to his son, Solomon, of the word of the LORD he received: ". . . I will give peace and quiet to Israel in [Solomon's] days" (1 Chr 22:9b). Under the leadership of Jonathan—during the time of the Maccabees—"Jonathan and his men [lived] in quiet and confidence" (1 Macc 9:58). Even the letter written by Queen Esther (Add Esth 8:8) in the name of King Artaxerxes of Persia—after the revelation of the plot to kill all the Jews—promises to take care "to render [the] kingdom quiet and peaceable for all" (Add Esth 16:8 [Esth E:8]).

Such quiet and peace enter the CB (NT) in the First Letter to Timothy. The anonymous author urges that supplications, prayers, intercessions, and thanksgivings be made for kings and all who are in high positions so that the recipients of the letter "may lead a quiet and peaceable life in all godliness and dignity" (1 Tim 2:2). The words in First Timothy echo those found in Paul's First Letter to the Thessalonians. The apostle urges his readers "to aspire to live quietly" (1 Thess 4:11). The phrase "peace and quiet" came into existence in the mid-1800s to refer to tranquility and freedom from disturbance. It can be considered redundant, unless the reader understands that quiet does not mean *lack of sound*, but, rather, connotes peacefulness. The intention of the phrase is to emphasize serene peace. The idiom is meant to indicate a period of time in which there are no disturbances. Thus, the Bible's use of the phrases *quiet and ease, quiet and confidence,* and *quiet and peaceable* are summarized in quiet and peace, the fullness of which exists in God alone.

Journal/Meditation: When have you most recently experienced quiet and peace? What triggered God's presence to you?

Prayer: I do not fear, O LORD, because I know you are with me to save me. Give me now the quiet and peace of your kingdom that I may look forward to its fullness in your presence forever. Amen.

Quiet Land

Scripture: "The whole earth is at rest and quiet . . . ." (Isa 14:7a)

Reflection: In the prophet Isaiah's mocking lament for the death of the king of Babylon, he declares that the whole earth is at rest and quiet because the greatest world power has been destroyed by the LORD (Isa 14:3–6). Without a king, the world is without war. Similarly, the author of the OT (A) First Book of Maccabees describes the earth becoming quiet before Alexander the Great (1 Macc 1:3b). Likewise, under the kingship of Demetrius I, "the land was quiet before him and . . . there was no opposition to him" (1 Macc 11:38). He was able to sit on the throne of his kingdom, according to First Maccabees, because "the land was quiet before him" (1 Macc 11:52). In a similar vein the chronicler records that the sons of the tribe of Simeon increased as they pastured their flocks to the west of the Judean heartland on the east side of the valley; there, they found rich, good pasture, "and the land was very broad, quiet, and peaceful" (1 Chr 4:40). Likewise, the chronicler records that "the realm of [King] Jehoshaphat [of Judah, 870–849 BCE] was quiet, for God gave him rest all around" (2 Chr 20:30).

Parks and conservation territories are probably the best places to find quiet land today, even though there may be sky noise from aircraft flying overhead. To those quiet lands can be added wilderness areas, where, except for the noises made by the animals that live there, the only sound may be planes leaving contrails in the sky. Many cities have created recreation trails that often follow creeks and rivers, but the sound of cars on city streets cannot be drowned by the trees. Pastures on rolling hills in the country can describe quiet land until the tractors appear to till the soil or cut the hay. Indeed, it may be close to impossible to find quiet land today!

Journal/Meditation: Where have you found quiet land? Describe it.

Prayer: O LORD, you set the earth on its foundations and boundaries for the waters. The quiet land is but one of your wisdom works. May my prayer give you glory and be pleasing to you as I rejoice in you as Father, Son, and Holy Spirit now and forever and ever. Amen.

Quiet People

Scripture: ". . . Jacob was a quiet man, living in tents." (Gen 25:27)

Reflection: The author of the HB (OT) book of Genesis presents the contrasts between the twins named Jacob and Esau (Gen 25:21–28), sons of Isaac, along with two versions of the story of how Jacob, the younger, got the birthright of Esau, the older (Gen 25:29–34; 27:1–45). While Jacob was a quiet man, he, nevertheless, lived up to the meanings of his name: (1) *he grips by the heel,* referring to his birth when he was gripping at Esau's heel (Gen 25:26) and his tendency to take advantage of others for his own self-interest (as, for example with Laban [Gen 30:35–43]); and (2) *he supplants* by stealing Esau's birthright (Gen 27:1–45). Biblically, it seems that quiet people are the victims of violence. The psalmist captures this idea, singing about his treacherous enemies who "do not speak peace, but they conceive deceitful words against those who are quiet in the land" (Ps 35:20).

For example, the Danites put to the sword the people who live in Laish who are described as "a people quiet and unsuspecting" (Judg 18:27). The prophet Ezekiel describes the people threatened by Gog as "quiet people who live in safety, all of them living without walls, and have no bars or gates" (Ezek 38:11). Even God himself declares, "My people will abide in a peaceful habitation, in secure dwellings and in quiet resting places" (Isa 32:18). Quiet people seem to be more susceptible to tragedy than to prosperity. Quiet people may desire to live peacefully, but enemies destroy them. Quiet people, like Jacob, are not found only in monasteries or living as hermits or anchorites; there are many people who live alone for whatever reason and are quiet people.

Journal/Meditation: What quiet people do you know? Make a list of their names and indicate the type of quietness each person demonstrates.

Prayer: O LORD, my God, do not let my treacherous enemies rejoice over me. Do not let them conceive deceitful words against those who live quietly in the land. Draw me ever deeper into the quiet shared by you, Father, with your Son, Jesus Christ, in the unity of the Holy Spirit forever and ever. Amen.

Quiet City

Scripture: O LORD, "Look on Zion, the city of our appointed festivals! Your eyes will see Jerusalem, a quiet habitation, an immovable tent, whose stakes will never be pulled up, and none of whose ropes will be broken." (Isa 33:20)

Reflection: After a time of war, especially one involving deportation of able-bodied citizens to the land of the conqueror, those remaining in the destroyed land need hope. And that is what the prophet Isaiah supplies for those left behind in Jerusalem after the destruction of the city in 587 BCE by King Nebuchadnezzar of Babylon and the deportation of its citizenry to his kingdom. Isaiah presents the hope in a prayer, which asks God to look on Zion, the hill upon which Jerusalem is built. It was once a quiet city in which many lived. Now, its walls are pulled down, but Isaiah offers hope that it will be one day an immovable tent with stakes that cannot be pulled out and ropes that cannot be torn apart. Such hope expressed over twenty-five hundred years ago still lingers in the air for modern Jerusalem, not to mention most modern cities.

The Second Book of Kings records a one-chapter story about Queen Athaliah—the daughter of King Ahab and Queen Jezebel of Israel—who had married King Joram (Jehoram) of Judah. Their son, Ahaziah, succeeded to the throne, but he was killed by King Jehu of Israel. Once Ahaziah is dead, Athaliah seizes the throne for herself and attempts to wipe out all the royal family, not knowing that Ahaziah's sister, Jehosheba, has taken her nephew, Joash, son of King Ahaziah, and kept him from being killed by Athaliah, who reigned over Israel for six or seven years. In the seventh year, Jehoida the priest led a military coup that enthroned Joash as King of Judah and put to death Athaliah (2 Kgs 11:1–19). According to the narrator, "All the people of the land rejoiced; and the city was quiet after Athaliah had been killed with the sword at the king's house" (2 Kgs 11:20). The same story appears in a slightly altered fashion in 2 Chronicles 22:10—23:21. The city of Jerusalem is not quiet until Athaliah, who was not eligible in a patriarchal culture to reign in Judah, is killed and the legitimate descendant of David is placed upon Judah's throne.

Journal/Meditation: What is the quietest city you have lived in? What made it so?

Prayer: O LORD, you are judge, ruler, and king, who saves those who place all their trust in you. Look upon me and the city (town, village) in which I live and make of it a quiet habitation today, tomorrow, and forever. Amen.

Quiet

Scripture: "Better is a dry morsel with quiet than a house full of feasting with strife." (Prov 17:1)

Reflection: The wisdom of the HB (OT) book of Proverbs presents a scale with a dry morsel of bread and quiet on one side and a house full of feasting and strife on the other. The scale tips in favor of the dry morsel of bread and quiet. In other words, it is better to eat in quiet a stale piece of bread than it is to eat in stress tasty banquet foods. In order to illustrate this bit of wisdom, Zophar the Naamathite, one of Job's friends, reminds Job that the wicked may rise high, ingesting wickedness like one eats delicious food, but they know "no quiet in their bellies; in their greed they let nothing escape" (Job 20:20). Indeed, ultimately they will get God's anger for their food, which will upset their stomachs (Job 20:23).

In the CB (NT) Acts of the Apostles, Paul is expelled from the temple in Jerusalem and a riot ensues. Ironically, he a Jew is protected by the Roman guard that has to carry him through the crowd to the barracks. A tribune permits him to address the crowd from the steps of the barracks. After motioning for silence, he addresses the people in Hebrew. According to Acts, "When they heard him addressing them in Hebrew, they became even more quiet" (Acts 22:2). The feast of strife that began in the temple with Paul's words that aroused the whole city was worse than being taken into quiet, protective custody by soldiers in the Roman cohort. Nevertheless, while the crowd is quiet, Paul presents his defense and the details of his encounter on the road to Damascus, but the crowd's violent response again forces the tribune to take Paul into the quiet barracks, where he learns that he is a Roman citizen (Acts 22:1–29). Better for Paul is imprisonment with quiet than a crowd full of strife.

Journal/Meditation: When have you experienced the quiet of protective custody—like being home alone or at the office alone—instead of strife—like family disagreements at home or office meetings that end in dissention?

Prayer: All-wise God, your wisdom transcends all natural boundaries and limits. Give me a greater appreciation for the time I spend with you and draw me deeper into the quiet of your divine life as Father, Son, and Holy Spirit now and forever. Amen.

Not Quiet Sea

Scripture: "[The sailors] said to [Jonah], 'What shall we do to you, that the sea may quiet down for us?' For the sea was growing more and more tempestuous. He said to them, 'Pick me up and throw me into the sea; then the sea will quiet down for you; for I know it is because of me that this great storm has come upon you.'" (Jonah 1:11–12)

Reflection: Everyone loves the HB (OT) book of Jonah. It is the fable about the LORD sending the prophet Jonah to Nineveh, an Assyrian city both feared and hated by the Israelites. In other words, Jonah is sent to his enemy to preach repentance. Unlike other prophetic books which narrate the prophet's acceptance of his call, Jonah creates a plan to escape his call. After boarding a ship heading in the opposite direction, Jonah and the sailors experience a great wind and a mighty storm at sea that threatens to destroy all onboard. The sea, especially when it is turbulent, represents chaos which only God can tame (Gen 1:1–13). Furthermore, the chaos of the sea is a sign of the chaos of Jonah's life; he is "fleeing from the presence of the LORD" (Jonah 1:10). The only way to still the sea—both the water and Jonah—is for the sailors to toss Jonah overboard. "So they picked Jonah up and threw him into the sea; and the sea ceased from its raging" (Jonah 1:15).

The same idea about the sea representing chaos is found in the prophet Jeremiah. In his speech about Damascus, he mentions two towns which "are confounded, for they have heard bad news; they melt in fear, they are troubled like the sea that cannot be quiet" (Jer 49:23). Job, too, expresses his distress using similar imagery: "I am not at ease, nor am I quiet; I have no rest; but trouble comes" (Job 3:26). In other words, Job curses the day he was born into the chaos of the world, which is known as suffering. The rich image of the sea as chaos or unquiet appears frequently in world literature, in film, in music, and in painting. It also appears in the lives of ordinary people—consciously or unconsciously. Often it is because one is attempting to flee from a decision that needs to be made; once made the chaos turns to quiet. Sometimes it is because a person is fleeing the presence of the LORD and needs to return to the only one who can still the sea (Ps 107:23–32).

Journal/Meditation: What has been your last chaos? What was it like? How did you quiet it?

Prayer: I call to you, O LORD, and you hear my voice. When the waters close in over me and the deep surrounds me, you deliver me from chaos just as you quiet the sea. Father, guide me with your Holy Spirit, who lives and reigns with you and your Son, Jesus Christ, to the quiet of your kingdom forever. Amen.

Quiet Spirit

Scripture: "The quiet words of the wise are more to be heeded than the shouting of a ruler among fools." (Eccl 9:17)

Reflection: The quiet words of the wise emerge from a quiet spirit; the shouting words of a ruler emerge from a disquiet spirit. The HB (OT) book of Judges describes the inhabitants of Laish as "living securely, . . . quiet and unsuspecting, lacking nothing on earth, and possessing wealth" (Judg 18:7a; cf. 18:27). In other words, they spoke quiet words of wisdom to each other out of their quiet spirit, while the Danites prepared to attack them, burn their city, and rename it Dan (Judg 18:27–29). The author of the First Letter of Peter, writing from a patriarchal culture point-of-view, exhorts wives to make their adornment "the inner self with the lasting beauty of a gentle and quiet spirit, which is very precious in God's sight" (1 Pet 3:4). Today, the desire for the inner beauty of a gentle and quiet spirit can be applied equally to husbands.

Because wisdom literature, such as that found in Ecclesiastes, is concerned with insight, instruction, and meditation on the practices and meaning of life, it focuses on the quiet words that emerge after a period of reflection, journaling, or mediation. Quiet words are not those spoken as an immediate response; quiet words are those which emerge from the depths of the inner self, the true self, the gentle and quiet spirit of a person. That is precious in God's sight because that is where a person touches the divine, where a person comes face to face with God, where a person is inspired, where the Spirit connects to spirit and only quiet, spiritual words are formed and spoken.

Journal/Meditation: What has been your most recent experience of deep, insightful, spiritual words emerging from your quiet spirit?

Prayer: Heavenly Father, in the quiet of your presence, words are heard that cannot be spoken. Strengthen my spiritual connection to your Holy Spirit that quiets my spirit and fills me with the wisdom of quiet words. Grant this in the name of your Son, Jesus Christ, who lives and reigns with you in absolute quiet now and forever. Amen.

4

Still and Calm

Be Still, Be Calm

Scripture: "Be still, and know that I am God! I am exalted among the nations, I am exalted in the earth." (Ps 46:10)

Reflection: Basically, God's words in Psalm 46 tell the singer, "Stop!" Then, once the psalmist has stopped, he or she acknowledges God's sovereignty. Similarly, the lyrics of Psalm 37 tell the hearers, "Be still before the LORD, and wait patiently for him" (Ps 37:7a). Keeping in mind that the coast represents the furthest limits of the world, the prophet Isaiah addresses those who live there, stating, "Be still, O inhabitants of the coast" (Isa 23:2a). The prophet Jeremiah addresses the LORD's sword, telling it, "Put yourself into your scabbard, rest and be still! (Jer 47:6b) However, Psalm 81 seeks help against enemies, beginning, "O God, do not keep silence; do not hold your peace or be still, O God!" (Ps 81:1), while the prophet Ezekiel records God's sword punishing the nations with whom Jerusalem was allied, as the LORD says: ". . . I will satisfy my fury on you, and my jealousy shall turn away from you; I will be calm, and will be angry no longer" (Ezek 16:42).

In the CB (NT), the author of Mark's Gospel records a story of Jesus and his disciples getting into a boat and crossing an unnamed body of water when a great windstorm arises, causing waves to swamp water into the boat. The disciples awaken Jesus, who is asleep; he rebukes the wind and says to the sea, "Peace! Be still!" (Mark 4:39a) The exorcised winds cease, the directly-addressed waves calm, and the disciples ask, "Who then is this, that even the wind and the sea obey him?" (Mark 4:41) The Matthean and Lukan versions of this story (Matt 8:23–27; Luke 8:22–25) omit Jesus' direct address to the sea. The point of being still, being calm—no matter how or why it is brought about—is to know God. Through the psalms and the prophets, the Israelites know God in stillness; through Jesus, the disciples know God through the calm.

Journal/Meditation: When have you experienced God's presence in stillness and calmness?

Prayer: O LORD, send your Holy Spirit into my life like a gentle breeze that stills and calms me to know that you alone are God. Grant me the grace to be still before you and to wait patiently for you. Hear me through Jesus Christ, your Son, who lives in stillness and calm with you and the Holy Spirit, one God, forever and ever. Amen.

Dead Calm

Scripture: ". . . [Jesus] said to [his disciples], 'Why are you afraid, you of little faith?' Then he got up and rebuked the winds and the sea; and there was a dead calm." (Matt 8:26)

Reflection: The phrase *dead calm* means *completely still with no waves and no wind. A perfectly flat sea with no waves is a dead calm.* The detail in Matthew's Gospel about the dead calm comes from his Markan source (Mark 4:35–41). After Jesus, who is asleep in the boat, is awakened by the disciples, who fear that their boat is going to sink, the Markan Jesus directly addresses the sea (Mark 4:39), thus imitating God (Gen 1:6–10; Ps 107:28–29). In Mark's Gospel, the narrator states that after Jesus addressed the sea "the wind ceased, and there was a dead calm" (Mark 4:39) before he asks his disciples, "Why are you afraid? Have you still no faith?" (Mark 4:40) Like the author of Matthew's Gospel, the author of Luke's Gospel uses his Markan source, but rewrites the account considerably (Luke 8:22–25). For example, they cross a lake. Jesus falls asleep while a windstorm sweeps down on the lake. When the disciples wake Jesus, they shout, "Master, Master we are perishing!" (Luke 8:24a) The narrator writes that Jesus rebuked the wind and the raging waves; once all ceased, "there was a calm" (Luke 8:24). Then Jesus asks them about their faith because they were afraid and amazed.

The variations in the account of the crossing of water with Jesus' calming of wind and sea found in Mark, Matthew, and Luke remind the reader that even inspired authors shape a story to fit the themes they want to illustrate in their books. Matthew's omniscient narrator removes Jesus' words in Mark, while the dead calm sea of Mark becomes merely a calm lake in Luke. The dead calm that Mark and Matthew present is a return to primeval times before creation began and "a wind from God swept over the face of the waters" (Gen 1:2). Jesus—in his Markan, Matthean, or Lukan versions—recreates the earth by his command. Fear is the response to the chaos of the sea for the disciples; faith is the response to the chaos of the sea for Jesus. No matter the response, he returns it to its primeval state: dead calm.

Journal/Meditation: Have you ever experienced a dead calm? Explain. Did it evoke fear or faith in you?

Prayer: Master, when I am perishing, command the winds to stop and the raging waves to cease. Bring me safely to shore with the breeze of the Holy Spirit. Lord Jesus Christ, carry my prayer to your Father, who re-creates through you and the Spirit now and forever. Amen.

Keep Still

Scripture: Moses said to the Israelites, "The LORD will fight for you, and you have only to keep still." (Exod 14:14)

Reflection: The Hebrews have escaped Egypt and are camped before the Red Sea when they see pharaoh and his army approaching. When they begin to panic, Moses tells them not to be afraid; the LORD will deliver them. In fact, using the image of divine warrior for God—that is, the LORD imaged as a warrior, leading heavenly armies into battle and fighting for the Israelites—Moses tells those following him to keep still. After crossing the Red Sea and observing the destruction of pharaoh's army in the waters, the Israelites sing, "Terror and dread fell upon them; by the might of [the LORD's] arm, they became still as a stone until [the LORD's] people . . . passed by, until the people whom [the LORD] acquired passed by" (Exod 15:16). The keeping still of the Israelites enables the becoming-still-as-a-stone of pharaoh's army.

In contrast to Moses' words to Israel to keep still are the LORD's words recorded by the prophet Isaiah. "For a long time I have held my peace, I have kept still and restrained myself; now I will cry out like a woman in labor, I will gasp and pant" (Isa 42:14). In other words, God can no longer keep still about his people who are slaves in Babylon. He shouts about not forsaking them and bringing them home (Isa 42:15—43:1). Once the exiles return to Jerusalem new troubles arise, primarily that of injustice. The wicked "are like the tossing sea that cannot keep still" records the prophet (Isa 57:20). The wicked are incapable of creating peace. Thus, there is a time to keep still and wait for the LORD to act, and, from God's point of view, there is a time to cease stillness and seek justice.

Journal/Meditation: When have you experienced the LORD rescuing you in the stillness? When have you experienced the LORD calling you to justice?

Prayer: I sing to you, LORD, for you have triumphed gloriously. You are my strength, my might, and my salvation. Help me to keep still in your presence that I may know what you ask of me through Jesus Christ my Lord. Amen.

Stand Still 1

Scripture: The LORD said to Joshua, "You are the one who shall command the priests who bear the ark of the covenant, 'When you come to the edge of the water of the Jordan, you shall stand still in the Jordan.' So when those who bore the ark had come to the Jordan, and the feet of the priests bearing the ark were dipped in the edge of the water, the waters flowing from above stood still. . . .'" (Josh 3:8, 15b–16a)

Reflection: To stand still, as do the priests carrying the ark of the covenant, is to cease all movement or activity and to prevent all further movement or activity. One stands still in order to wait for and, then, observe God's activity. Once the priests with the ark enter the Jordan River and stand still, the water imitates them; the water stands still. Just as the LORD made the waters of the Red Sea stand still so Moses could lead the Israelites through it, so does God make the waters of the Jordan stand still so Joshua, Moses' successor, can lead the Israelites into the promised land. In a similar way, Jonathan, son of King Saul, tells his armor-bearer how to determine whether the LORD is acting for him when approaching a garrison of Philistines: "If they say to us, 'Wait until we come to you,' then we will stand still in our place, and we will not go up to them. But if they say, 'Come up to us,' then we will go up; for the LORD has given them into our hand. That will be the sign for us" (1 Sam 14:9–10). The Philistines invite them to come to them, and Jonathan and his armor-bearer kill about twenty men (1 Sam 14:14) because "the LORD [had] given them into the hand of Israel" (1 Sam 14:12b). Likewise, while "all Judah stood before the LORD" (2 Chr 20:13), Jahaziel tells King Jehoshaphat, "[The imminent] battle is not for you to fight; take your position, stand still, and see the victory of the LORD on your behalf, O Judah and Jerusalem" (2 Chr 20:17a).

In the face of death about all one can do is to stand still. The narrator of the Second Book of Samuel tells a story about Asahel, who is faithful to David, being killed by Abner, who is faithful to Ishbaal, son of Saul (2 Sam 2:18–23c). ". . . [A]ll those who came to the place where Asahel had fallen and died, stood still" (2 Sam 2:23d). Likewise, when inquiring about his son Absalom—who is dead (2 Sam 18:14)—the messenger Ahimaaz is told by King David, "'Turn aside, and stand here.' So he turned aside, and stood still" (2 Sam 18:30). Also, Eliphaz the Temanite tells Job about a vision he has during the night which informs him of the insignificance of human beings: "A spirit glided past my face; the hair of my flesh bristled. It stool still, but I could not discern its appearance. A form was before my eyes; there was silence, then I heard a voice" (Job 4:15–16). It's not a voice, but a trumpet which keeps the horse from standing still, according to God (Job 39:24). Thus, to stand still is to cease all movement or activity and to prevent all further movement or activity in order to observe God's activity.

Journal/Meditation: When have you stood still and observed God's activity?

Prayer: O LORD, God of my ancestors, in your hand is power and might, so that no one is able to withstand you. Send your Holy Spirit to calm me that I may stand still before you and witness your mighty deeds. Hear me through Jesus Christ my Lord. Amen.

Stand Still 2

Scripture: "At that time [when the Lord draws near to visit the inhabitants of the earth] . . . the springs of the fountains shall stand still, so that for three hours they shall not flow." (2 Esd 6:24)

Reflection: In the apocalyptic and apocryphal book of Second Esdras, a voice from heaven tells Ezra about the end of the world. One of the signs of its end is the standing still of the springs of the fountains, which is a reversal of the natural order of the earth. Likewise, the Prayer of Azariah in the OT (A) book of Daniel presents a reversal of the natural order as three young Jews walk around in the midst of flames, singing hymns to God and blessing the Lord. The narrator of the event notes, "Azariah [, one of the three men,] stood still in the fire and prayed aloud" (Sg Three 1:2 [Dan 3:25]).

In the CB (NT), Jesus is portrayed as reversing the natural order of the world after standing still. The author of Mark's Gospel narrates a story about a blind beggar named Bartimaeus sitting by the Jericho roadside when Jesus of Nazareth is passing by. The beggar shouts to the Son of David, seeking mercy. The crowd sternly orders him to be quiet, but he just shouts all the louder. "Jesus stood still" (Mark 10:49) and told the crowd to bring the blind man to him. Once he acknowledges that the blind man sees—that is, he has faith that Jesus' disciples do not have—he heals his blindness with sight, and the once-blind man follows Jesus (Mark 10:46–52). The author of Matthew's Gospel changes his Markan source by removing the named, blind Bartimaeus and replacing him with two, unnamed blind men before whom Jesus stands still (Matt 20:29–34). Not only does Matthew double Markan singular characters, Matthew also doubles stories, such as another story about two blind men Jesus heals in a house (Matt 9:27–31). The author of Luke's Gospel removes the name of the blind man and expands the account of Jesus standing still to heal in order to emphasize Jesus' role to give sight to the blind (Luke 18:35–43; 4:18b). Luke also portrays the bearers of the bier with the dead body of the son of the widow of Nain standing still after Jesus touches it and brings the dead man back to life (Luke 7:11–17); here, Jesus is fulfilling his role of bringing good news to the poor (Luke 4:18a) and reversing the natural order of the earth. Finally, when the risen Jesus joins two disciples on their way to the village of Emmaus, Luke states, "They stood still, looking sad" (Luke 24:17b); resurrection reverses the natural order of the world. Thus, Jesus' standing still, like the standing still of springs of fountains and a young man in a fiery furnace, reverses the natural order of the world.

Journal/Meditation: When have you stood still and experienced the reversal of the natural order of the world?

Prayer: Blessed are you, O Lord, my God; worthy are you of all praise, and glorious is your name forever. The springs of water praise you. The fire blesses you. And Jesus, your Son, extols you. I stand still and give thanks to you, Father, for your mercy endures forever. Amen.

Silent and Still

Scripture: "I was silent and still; I held my peace to no avail; my distress grew worse . . . ." (Ps 39:2)

Reflection: The psalmist begins by singing to himself and recounting how he promised to keep his mouth muzzled (Ps 39:1). He achieves silence and stillness, but his distress takes over and grows worse. He describes his condition as being like his heart is on fire; he is compelled to speak to God about the transience of human life (Ps 39:3–6). Similarly, the prophet Jeremiah describes his experience of having to speak to the Israelites about the destruction of Jerusalem by the Babylonians (Jer 20:4–6). In the last of what are known as five confessions, Jeremiah, like the psalmist, vows not to speak in the LORD's name because his message is always violence and destruction (Jer 20:8). However, after making the vow, the prophet discovers that within him "there is something like a burning fire shut up in [his] bones" and he is "weary with holding it in" and he cannot contain it any longer (Jer 20:9). Jeremiah's silence and stillness explode with divine words of terror.

The psalmist and Jeremiah can be contrasted to the high priest Simon in the OT (A) Third Book of Maccabees. Ptolemy IV Philopator is king of Egypt (221–204 BCE), and he decides to enter the Holy of Holies of the Jerusalem Temple. Only the high priest is allowed to do this once a year (Exod 30:10; Heb 9:7). The Jewish community declares that this action will profane the temple (3 Macc 1:29). So, "the high priest Simon, facing the sanctuary, bending his knees and extending his hands with calm dignity, prayed . . ." (3 Macc 2:1). His silent and still stance enables him to voice a nineteen verse prayer (3 Macc 2:2–20). After reminding the Lord of all his previous marvelous works for the Jews, he asks for help to stop the audacious and profane Ptolemy from violating the holy place on earth dedicated to God's name (3 Macc 2:14). God responds to Simone's silent and still prayer by striking Ptolemy with paralysis in his limbs and mouth (3 Macc 2:21–24). Thus, because Ptolemy can no longer walk or talk, the temple is spared from profanation. In calm, aided by silence and stillness,

Simon intercedes with God on behalf of his people, and the Lord answers his prayer.

Journal/Meditation: When have you experienced your silence and stillness erupting into fiery talk or prayer? When have you experience your calmness in prayer being answered by God?

Prayer: Hear my prayer, O LORD, for I know that I am but a passing guest in your sight. I sing to you, king of the heavens and sovereign of all creation, because you overtake me with your mercies and you deliver me through Jesus Christ now and forever. Amen.

Sit Still, Lie Still

Scripture: "[Sisera] sank, he fell, he lay still at [Jael's] feet; at her feet he sank, he fell; where he sank, there he fell dead." (Judg 5:27)

Reflection: In the HB (OT) book of Judges, there is a story about Sisera, commander of King Jabin of Canaan's army at the time when Deborah, a prophetess, was judging Israel (Judg 4:1–5). God informs Deborah of his plan to eliminate Jabin's army, and Deborah passes on this information to Barak, another judge of Israel. Barak assembles his own army and defeats all of Jabin's except for Sisera, who escapes (Judg 4:6–16). While running away, Sisera flees into the tent of Jael; she recognizes him and, under the guise of hospitality, invites him into her tent and covers him with a rug. Then, she takes a tent peg and, with hammer in hand, drives it into his temple, killing him (Judg 4:17–24). Then, she and Barak sing a thirty-one verse song (Judg 5:1–31) about Jael's victory over Sisera, who lay dead still at her feet. Her song mentions the tribe of Asher, which "sat still at the coast of the sea" (Judg 5:17b). In a similar vein, the prophet Ezekiel presents the last of seven oracles about pharaoh and Egypt. The LORD tells the prophet to send them down to the world below (Ezek 32:18). In Sheol mighty chiefs will say, "They have come down, they lie still, the uncircumcised, killed by the sword" (Ezek 32:21b). Isaiah has no kind words for Egypt either; after considering Egypt's lack of help given to King Hezekiah (716–687 BCE), Isaiah calls her "Rahab who sits still"

(Isa 30:7). The prophet is either calling Egypt a dragon monster of ancient time or referring to the sphinx. In either case, he is acknowledging the worthless and empty help of Egypt, that is, the lack of protection received by Hezekiah for Judah after watching Assyria destroy Israel.

The prophet Jeremiah takes the reader back to the time of the Babylonian exile. While the exiles are in captivity or getting ready to go into it, they ask, "Why do we sit still?" (Jer 8:14a) Indeed, why do they sit still when the LORD has doomed them to perish (Jer 8:14b). Biblically, such inactivity as sitting still or lying still signals death in some way. Sisera laid still and died at Jael's hand. Asher sat still near the northwestern coast and was destroyed by the Assyrians. Egypt is sent to Sheol because it fails to help Hezekiah defeat his enemy. And the Jews moved to Babylon sit still in a foreign land; their captivity is a type of death. Thus, sitting still or lying still inaugurates dying in some form, and sometimes the dying is literal. As a way of life, spirituality is often about sitting still or lying still in order to be transformed.

Journal/Meditation: When have you discovered transformation because you sat still or laid still?

Prayer: O LORD, when you went to Mount Tabor, the earth trembled, the heavens poured water, and the earth quaked before you. At your command, Jael put her hand to the tent peg and struck Sisera, your enemy, a blow. Grant that I may be counted among your friends, who are like the sun as it rises in its might now and forever. Amen.

Still Sun and Moon

Scripture: ". . . Joshua spoke to the LORD; and he said in the sight of Israel, 'Sun, stand still at Gibeon, and Moon, in the valley of Aijalon.' And the sun stood still, and the moon stopped, until the nation took vengeance on their enemies. . . . The sun stopped in midheaven, and did not hurry to set for about a whole day." (Josh 10:12–13ac)

Reflection: Moses' successor, Joshua, who is camped in Gilgal, receives word from the Gibeonites that the Amorites are getting ready to attack them. So, Joshua gathers an army and marches
from Gilgal to Gibeon. "The LORD said to Joshua, 'Do not fear
them, for I have handed them over to you, not one of them shall
stand before you'" (Josh 10:8). The narrator of the HB (OT) book
of Joshua states: ". . . [T]he LORD threw them into a panic before
Israel, who inflicted a great slaughter on them at Gibeon, chased
them . . . , struck them down . . . , [and] threw down huge [hail]
stones from heaven on them . . ." (Josh 10:9–11). Of course, because Joshua is modeled on Moses, the panic in which he throws
the enemy is like the panic into which he threw the Egyptian army
when Israel crossed the Red Sea (Exod 15:24). The hailstones are
like the plague that the LORD rained upon Egypt before pharaoh
let the Israelites leave (Exod 9:22–26).

The book of Joshua also recounts one of Joshua's more famous
deeds. Joshua requests that the LORD give him extended daylight.
And the LORD grants his request by making the sun stand still at
noon and delay its setting. However, the poem embedded in the
text comes from the no longer extant Book of Jashar (Josh 10:13b);
the poet addresses the sun and the moon, and tells them to stand
still. In essence, the poet calls upon the sun and the moon to freeze
in stunned amazement at Israel's victory, similar to the amazement
expressed in the song of Moses and the Israelites after the defeat
of pharaoh and his army (Exod 15:16). Then, the narrator declares
that the sun stood still, and the moon stopped until Israel defeated
the Amorites (Josh 10:13a). The OT (A) book of Sirach (Ecclesiasticus) rehearses this event, asking, "Was it not through [Joshua]
that the sun stood still and one day became as long as two? He
called upon the Most High, the Mighty One, when enemies
pressed him on every side, and the great Lord answered him with
hailstones of mighty power" (Sir 46:4–5). The prophet Habakkuk
records a prayer-psalm praising the LORD's theophanic presence
which caused the sun to raise high its hands and the moon to stand
still in its exalted place (Hab 3:10b–11a).

Journal/Meditation: To what natural phenomena do you think the biblical texts are referring? How do a still sun and moon manifest the divine?

Prayer: O LORD, I have heard of your renown, and I stand in awe, O LORD, of your work. Fill me with your rays of grace, like sun bolts covering the earth. Grant that I may stand still in exultation before you, like the moon, as the light of your Son, Jesus Christ, guides me to you today, tomorrow, and forever. Amen.

Calm and Still

Scripture: "Those who are patient stay calm until the right moment, and then cheerfulness comes back to them. They hold back their words until the right moment; then the lips of many tell of their good sense." (Sir 1:23–24)

Reflection: The wisdom found in the OT (A) book of Sirach is echoed in the HB (OT) book of Proverbs. Sirach praises those who patiently stay calm by not speaking until the right moment. Seizing the moment, they calmly and patiently speak words of wisdom which bring them cheerfulness and the praise of others for their good sense. The book of Proverbs presents the same wisdom from a negative point of view: "Those who are hot-tempered stir up strife, but those who are slow to anger calm contention" (Prov 15:18). In Job's final speech, he states that he went looking for good, but evil came instead. He waited for light, but all he got was darkness (Job 20:26). "My inward parts are in turmoil, and are never still," he says; "days of affliction come to meet me" (Job 30:27). In other words, Job's patient calmness did not bring him cheerfulness in his suffering.

The chronicler narrates how the land was still during the reign of King Asa of Judah (911–870 BCE) because Asa himself was still, doing what was good and right in the sight of the LORD (2 Chr 14:2). According to the chronicler, "In his days the land had rest for ten years" (2 Chr 14:1b). "And the kingdom had rest under him. He built fortified cities in Judah while the land had rest" (2 Chr 14:5b–6a). The land at rest means that there is no war, "for the LORD gave [Asa] peace" (2 Chr 14:6b). In the words of the prophet Azariah, the LORD is with Asa while he is with God. As long as Asa seeks the LORD, he is found, but if Asa abandons the LORD, the LORD abandons him (2 Chr 15:2). In other words, when the land is calm, it is because Asa is calm; when the land is still, it is because Asa is still. Asa was patiently calm until the right moment, and then the cheerfulness of the defeat of his enemies came to him. He held back his words until the right moment; then he told of how the LORD his God was with him. However, once he stopped relying on the LORD, war came to his once-rested land (2 Chr 16:1–14).

Journal/Meditation: When have you been patient, staying calm until the right moment, and then cheerfulness came to you? When have you held back your words until the right moment, and then others praised your good sense?

Prayer: O LORD, my God, I rely on you, and in your name I come into your presence seeking your mercy. You alone know that my heart is true. You, whose eyes range throughout the entire earth, strengthen me in your service now and forever and ever. Amen.

Calm Harbor, Still Waters

Scripture: "How then can one fail to confess the sovereignty of right reason over emotion in those who were not turned back by fiery agonies? For just as towers jutting out over harbors hold back the threatening waves and make it calm for those who sail into the inner basin, so the seven-towered right reason of the youths, by fortifying the harbor of religion, conquered the tempest of the emotions." (4 Macc 13:5–7)

Reflection: While the Fourth Book of Maccabees was never considered to be canonical, it was often included in biblical manuscripts because it praised the martyrdom of seven brothers (4 Macc 8:1), an account that is garnered from OT (A) Second Maccabees 7:1–42. In Fourth Maccabees, the seven brothers are presented as philosophical examples of how "devout reason is sovereign over the emotions" (4 Macc 1:1). According to the second-century Jewish author, "by reason, which is praised before God, they prevailed over their emotions" (4 Macc 13:3). He adds, "The supremacy of the mind over these [emotions] cannot be overlooked, for the brothers mastered both emotions and pains" (4 Macc 13:4). Thus, the seven brothers conquered their tempestuous emotions using reason and sailed into the calm harbor of their Jewish faith; they are like towers jutting out over harbors that hold back the threatening waves and make it calm for those who sail into the inner basin (4 Macc 13:6–7).

As the author of Fourth Maccabees states, reason is praised before God (4 Macc 13:3), who leads the psalmist beside still waters (Ps 23:2), providing him drink. Another psalmist makes clear that the LORD rules the raging of the sea; thus, when its waves rise, the LORD stills them (Ps 89:9). In another psalm the LORD makes the storm still and the waves of the sea hushed (Ps 107:29). Because the sea represents chaos in biblical literature, only God can calm it. This is why the author of Mark's Gospel presents Jesus being like God and saying to the sea, "Peace! Be still!" (Mark 4:39a) When God utters judgment from the heavens, where he dwells, the earth fears and is still (Ps 76:8). However, the psalmist can ask God not to keep silence, not to hold his peace, and not to be still when he is facing enemies (Ps 83:1). A calm harbor and still waters may indicate the power of reason over emotions philosophically, but they also indicate the LORD's power over everything he created.

Journal/Meditation: Have you ever experienced a calm harbor and still waters while being on a ship of any size? Have you ever experienced the raging of the sea while being on a ship of any size? What emotions accompanied your experience? How did you calm your emotions?

Prayer: You, LORD, are my shepherd, and you lead me to still waters. Even when I travel over raging seas, you are with me. Bestow upon me your goodness and mercy all the days of my life, and grant that I may one day dwell in your house forever and ever. Amen.

Calm Anger and Wrath

Scripture: "There are winds created for vengeance, and in their anger they can dislodge mountains; on the day of reckoning they will pour out their strength and calm the anger of their Maker." (Sir 39:28)

Reflection: The verse above from the OT (A) book of Sirach (Ecclesiasticus) serves as an introduction to the author's reflection about what calms God's anger. The reader must keep in mind that the attributes of people are applied to God in biblical literature. Thus, just as people experience anger, so the biblical writer presumes that the divine does too. This is based on an understanding that if people are made in the image and likeness of God (Gen 1:27), and if people experience anger, then God must experience anger. According to the author of Sirach, what calms God's anger are the winds of vengeance! He writes about the vengeance (plagues) the winds bring to the Egyptians keeping the Hebrews in slavery: fire, hail, famine, pestilence, the fangs of wild animals, scorpions, vipers, and the sword (Sir 39:29–30). According to Sirach, "They take delight by doing [the Lord's] bidding, always ready for his service on earth; and when their time comes they never disobey his command" (Sir 39:31).

In the last section of the book, Sirach presents a hymn in honor of ancestors. One ancestor mentioned is Elijah, who, at the appointed time is destined "to calm the wrath of God before it breaks out in fury" (Sir 48:10a). This is not exactly what the prophet Malachi says: "Lo, I will send you the prophet Elijah before the great and terrible day of the LORD comes" (Mal 4:5 [3:23]). The day of the Lord refers to the LORD's manifestation of himself in power and glory, that is, a theophany, by overturning all Israel's enemies and establishing his people supreme. The phrase is meant to present God's power to judge and to save. According to Sirach, Elijah will be sent to calm God's wrath—calm the anger of his Maker—before judgment begins.

Journal/Meditation: Do you consider God to possess anger and wrath? If so, how? If not, why not? What calms your anger and wrath?

Prayer: O LORD, do not rebuke me in your anger or discipline me in your wrath. Remember your mercies, be gracious to me, and show me your steadfast love today, tomorrow, and forever. Amen.

Hush

Scripture: ". . . Paul stood on the steps and motioned to the people for silence; and when there was a great hush, he addressed them in the Hebrew language . . . ." (Acts 21:40)

Reflection: The word *hush*, meaning *to be quiet*, is used only two times in the Bible. After being taken into protective custody by a Roman tribune to protect Paul from the Jews, who are upset with his preaching, Paul gets the permission of the tribune to speak to the people before he is brought into the barracks (Acts 21:27–39). Motioning with his hand for the crowd to be quiet, and then waiting for a great hush—such as Shhh!—Paul begins to explain himself, by giving a narrative about his own experience of the risen Christ (Acts 22:1–21) before the tribune has to save him from the crowd by bringing him into the barracks (Acts 22:22–29).

The other biblical use of the word *hush* is found in the HB (OT) book of Amos. After a rather scathing indictment of Samaria, the capital of the Northern Kingdom of Israel, Amos announces the fall of that city and kingdom and the exile that will ensue (Amos 6:7–8). Then, he explains how this will take place: "If ten people remain in one house, they shall die. And if a relative, one who burns the dead, shall take up the body to bring it out of the house, and shall say to someone in the innermost parts of the house, 'Is anyone else with you?' the answer will come, 'No.' Then the relative shall say, 'Hush! We must not mention the name of the LORD" (Amos 6:9–10). After explaining that Samaria and Israel will be destroyed, like a cameraman Amos zooms in on a scene taking place in the city within a single house where ten people have huddled together for survival. He hypothesizes that the relative in the house of another in the house dies and is carried outside to be cremated at this time of war to prevent the spread of plague or infection. The person carrying the corpse asks loud enough to be heard by anyone near the back of the house, "Is anyone else with you?" (Amos 6:10a) The question is ambiguous because it can refer to anyone else alive or any other dead. No matter the case, the answer is heard, "No" (Amos 6:10a). Then, the relative carrying the corpse out of the house commands the person in the innermost part of the house to refrain from any further conversation: "Hush" (Amos 6:10b). The name of the LORD is not to be mentioned because it is he who has decreed this destruction, and those who are still alive may die. In other words, one person tells the other one, "Do not say another word in the place where God has decreed death, or we, too, may be stuck down."

Journal/Meditation: When have you most recently used the word *hush*? What did you mean by using it? What did the other person understand you to mean by your use of it?

Prayer: O Lord GOD, you swore by yourself that the great house of Israel would be shattered to bits, and that the little house of its residents would be broken into pieces. Keep me from that fate, and guide me in your ways. Hush me that I may hear your word spoken through your Son, Jesus Christ, in the unity of the Holy Spirit forever and ever Amen.

5

Transfigured by Silence

THE GOAL OF THIS book on biblical silence is transfiguration. When finishing its processes, the reader should be altered, changed, transformed. It is very hard to find silence, a silent place, quiet, or a place of still and calm. However, silence enables limited awareness caused by sound (noise) to be raised to great awareness of the divine presence—no matter how one names it—in silence. This greater awareness acknowledges the divine presence in one's midst—before, behind, above, below, and to the side—what Paul in his First Letter to the Corinthians calls all in all (15:28). Hopefully, the biblical material, the reflections, the journal/mediation questions, and the prayers in this book have sparked your creativity.

When writing about being altered, changed, transformed by silence, the key word is transfigured, which denotes the transformation in appearance of someone revealing great spirituality, that is, great connection of spirit to Spirit. The word also refers to the three accounts of Jesus' theophany—manifestation of God—in the synoptic gospels (Mark, Matthew, Luke). Those narratives, as we will see, mostly occur in divine silence.

Transfiguration according to Mark

The oldest narrative of the transfiguration of Jesus found in Mark's Gospel (9:2–10) occurs "six days" (Mark 9:2) after Jesus had been teaching on the way to Caesarea Philippi. The biblical number six does not refer to the amount of six days, but denotes that the event is incomplete.[1] The event is incomplete because it is a post-resurrection story. Employing a literary device known as the messianic secret throughout his work—those who should know who Jesus is do not, and those who should not know who he is do—the author of Mark creates the transfiguration narrative to be a resurrection statement. Furthermore, since this author ends his work with the women leaving the empty tomb and saying nothing to anyone (Mark 16:8), resulting in the culmination of his powerlessness theme, he cannot add a story about Jesus appearing to anyone because that would return him to a theme of power which he successfully stopped at Mark 8:31. Thus, everything in the transfiguration story points toward it serving as a post-resurrection account even though it is located in the middle of the gospel!

For example, there are three sets of three: (1) Peter, James, and John (Mark 9:2); (2) Elijah, Moses, and Jesus (Mark 9:4); (3) Peter's desire to make three dwellings (Mark 9:5). Three refers to the spiritual order; it indicates the divine presence.[2] There is no doubt that this is thrice the divine presence by its repetition. The event takes place on a high mountain (Mark 9:2), an element of most theophanic experiences.[3] This alone is enough without recognizing that Elijah encountered God on Mount Horeb (Sinai) (1 Kgs 19:11b–13a), and before him, Moses encountered God on Mount Horeb (Sinai) (Exod 19:16–19). Since Elijah and Moses have been dead for a very long time when Jesus comes onto the scene, it is clear that this story is meant to serve as a portal with a view into eternal life on the other side of death. The story is incomplete (6 days) because Jesus has not yet died and been raised to that eternal

1. Boyer, *Divine Presence*, 14.

2. Ibid., 11.

3. Ibid., 1.

life of which the reader gets a peek. As the Markan Jesus makes clear later in the text, God is not the God of the dead, but of the living (Mark 12:27).

Jesus' dazzling white clothes (Mark (9:3) indicate that he is divine, since white is the color proper to deity.[4] Furthermore, Elijah and Moses are alive in a type of life that awaits Jesus after his death. The narrator of Mark's transfiguration account explains that Peter did not know what to say because he and his two companions were terrified, another usual element of theophanies.[5] The cloud that overshadows all of them (Mark 9:7) is none other than the LORD,[6] and the voice that is heard coming from it confirms that, indeed, God is speaking (Mark 9:7).[7] Then, just as the scene suddenly had begun, it suddenly ends (Mark 9:8). The fact that the author of Mark's Gospel considers this to be a post-resurrection narrative is found in the verses that follow. "As they were coming down the mountain, [Jesus] ordered [Peter, James, and John] to tell no one about what they had seen, until the Son of Man had risen from the dead" (Mark 9:9). The author also narrates: "So they kept the matter to themselves, questioning what this rising from the dead could mean" (Mark 9:10). This is one of the few—if not the only time—Jesus' Markan disciples actually do what Jesus tells them to do!

It is very important to note that in this nine-verse story there are only two lines of monologue: Peter's words to Jesus (Mark 9:5) and God's words to Peter, James, and John (Mark 9:7). All else occurs in silence! Garvey refers to the transfiguration account as depicting "the flesh deified."[8] He explains: "That deification is shown to us in the revelation of the uncreated light of Mount Tabor . . . ,"[9] the traditional name given to the unnamed mountain in the biblical texts. In Mark's Gospel, the transfiguration narrative is meant

4. Ibid., 113.
5. Ibid., 31.
6. Ibid., 34.
7. Ibid., 26.
8. Garvey, *Wonder*, 75.
9. Ibid.

to give the reader a peek into resurrected life with Elijah, Moses, and Jesus on the other side of death in the presence of the divine.

Transfiguration according to Matthew

While the transfiguration narrative found in Mark's Gospel presents transformation in silence, the author of Matthew's Gospel presents it as metamorphosis—a complete change of physical form. He does this because he understands the narrative that he found in Mark's Gospel to be a prediction of what will happen to Jesus. The author of Matthew's Gospel loves to use the prediction-fulfillment theme. Thus, the transfiguration predicts Jesus' resurrection, and the two post-resurrection appearances of Jesus fulfill it (Matt 28:1–20). Thus, the author makes only minor changes in the story he found in Mark's Gospel.

Matthew emphasizes the metamorphosis of Jesus by adding that "his face shone like the sun" (Matt 17:2). He reverses the order of naming Elijah and Moses as Mark presents them as Moses and Elijah (Matt 17:3) because he understands Jesus to be a new Moses (Matt 1:13–23) who gives five major discourses in imitation of Moses, who is attributed with writing the five books of Torah (Genesis, Exodus, Leviticus, Numbers, and Deuteronomy) (Matt 5:1—7:29; 10:1—11:1; 13:1–53; 18:1—19:1; 24:1—26:1). Peter's line is lengthened by his comment about how good it is to be there (Matt 17:4), but that line and the voice from the cloud remain the only two lines spoken by any character during the event. The disciples' fear is calmed by Jesus touch, and a new line is provided for Jesus to speak (Matt 17:7). And the omniscient narrator's line in Mark about Jesus telling the disciples to say nothing about their experience on the mountain is replaced in Matthew with Jesus' direct address about telling no one of the vision until after the Son of Man has been raised from the dead (Matt 17:9). Matthew has removed Mark's comment about the disciples keeping all this to themselves. Thus, while Mark's basic transfiguration remains intact, Matthew has further emphasized the connection between

Jesus and Moses and their mountaintop theophanies in less silence than Mark.

Seemingly using Matthew's account as his basis, the anonymous author of the Second Letter of Peter narrates the event from the perspective of being an eyewitness (2 Pet 1:16, 18). He understands that the transfiguration was Jesus' reception of honor and glory from God the Father when the voice was conveyed to him by the Majestic Glory (2 Pet 1:17). The author interprets the transfiguration as a prediction of Jesus return in glory (2 Pet 1:16). The only speaking part in the narrative is given to God the Father (2 Pet 1:17).

Transfiguration according to Luke

As did Matthew before him, the author of Luke's Gospel found Mark's transfiguration narrative and understood it as a peek into perfect, eternal life, a foretelling of future events, and an example of keeping silent. First, the peek into perfect, eternal life is signaled by the narrator's statement that it was about eight days after Jesus had taught that there were some standing and listening to him who would not taste death before they saw the kingdom of God (Luke 9:27). The author of Luke's Gospel places the event after about eight days because eight is a perfect number; it represents fullness in God's sight.[10] To further emphasize the peek into life on the other side of death—obviously presented by the presence of Moses and Elijah in glory seen by Peter, James, and John (Luke 9:31–32)—Luke portrays Jesus praying (Luke 9:29), a motif used throughout this work.

Second, the foretelling of future events is discovered in the unique Lukan note about the discussion between Moses and Elijah about Jesus "departure, which he was about to accomplish at Jerusalem" (Luke 9:31). The Greek word translated as departure is exodus, and it refers both to Jesus' departure from death to resurrection (Luke 24:1–49), and, again, unique in Luke to his

---

10. Boyer, *Divine Presence*, 15.

ascension into heaven (Luke 24:50–53; Acts 1:1–11). Shortly after the narration of the transfiguration, the Lukan narrator states: "When the days drew near for [Jesus] to be taken up, he set his face to go to Jerusalem" (Luke 9:51). To his Markan source, the author of Luke's Gospel adds material about Peter, James, and John being weighed down with sleep, but they managed to stay awake (Luke 9:32). Their being sleepy indicates that they have entered a trance like the first man (Gen 2:21) and Abram (Gen 15:12) when they experienced God.

Third, the story is an example of keeping silent. The narrator makes that clear, when he explains that Peter, James, and John "kept silent and in those days told no one any of the things they had seen" (Luke 9:36b). Furthermore, Luke adds an important note about Jesus being found alone after the voice has spoken (Luke 9:36a); this further emphasizes the solitudinous silence that has transfigured not only Jesus, but Peter, James and John. As in Mark's Gospel, only Peter (Luke 9:33) and the voice from the cloud have lines to speak (Luke 9:35).

Others Transfigured by Silence

Other that the ones describing Jesus' transfiguration, there are narratives—not biblically obvious—that are, nevertheless, transformation accounts. The author of John's Gospel identifies one when he writes that the Word who was God became flesh and lived among people (John 1:1, 14). The invisible Word was transfigured into visible flesh. His visible flesh revealed divine glory as of a father's only son (John 1:14).

In his Letter to the Galatians, Paul states that the gospel proclaimed to him is not of human origin; he received it through a revelation of Jesus Christ (Gal 1:11). Paul explains that God chose to reveal his Son to him so that Paul might proclaim him among the Gentiles (Gal 1:16). That revelation transfigured Paul, as he states about himself: "The one who formerly was persecuting us is now proclaiming the faith he once tried to destroy" (Gal 1:23). The best examples of Paul being transfigured by silence is presented three times in the CB (NT) Acts of the Apostles. The first is narrated in the form of a theophany, featuring light (Acts 9:3) and a voice that reveals itself as coming from Jesus (Acts 9:5). As noted above, the light and the voice reveal divinity in a silent transfiguring experience. Those traveling with Paul could hear the voice, but they could see no one (Acts 9:7). Neither can Paul see for three divine days (Acts 9:3). A disciple in Jerusalem, named Ananias, is told by the Lord that Paul has been transfigured (Acts 9:13–16). Ananias finds Paul, lays his hands on him so he is filled with the Holy Spirit, and tells him that it is the Lord Jesus who appeared to him on the road; then, Paul regains his sight (Acts 9:17–18). The proof of his transfiguration is his proclamation: "[Jesus] is the Son of God" (Acts 9:20).

Later in the Acts when Paul is in Jerusalem he rehashes his transfiguring experience to the Jews about the great light and the voice of Jesus of Nazareth (Acts 22:6, 8), as noted above; in this account his companions can see the light, but they cannot hear the voice (Acts 22:9). The Lukan Paul states that he could not see because of the brightness of the light (Acts 22:11). However, he does explain that once he got to Jerusalem he fell into a trance, saw Jesus, and heard him sending him to the Gentiles (Acts 22:17–21).

In the third account of Paul's experience of transfiguration, the apostle narrates it to King Agrippa II (Acts 26:1–32). He explains how "at midday along the road" he "saw a light from heaven, brighter than the sun, shining around [him] and [his] companions" (Acts 26:13). Then, he heard a voice whose speaker identified himself as Jesus (Acts 26:14–17). The man who had been against Jesus of Nazareth (Acts 26:9) is silently transformed by his heavenly vision (Acts 26:19) into the apostle to the Gentiles. As in the other accounts of Paul's transformation, the theophanic light and the voice signal the change.

In his First Letter to the Corinthians, Paul indicates that he has seen Jesus the Lord (1 Cor 9:1). Later in the same letter, he states that Christ appeared to him (1 Cor 15:8), who had been a persecutor of the church of God (1 Cor 15:9). "But by the grace of God I am what I am, and his grace toward me has not been in vain," he adds (1 Cor 15:10a). In other words, Paul has been transfigured by silent grace, which one day will result in the transformation of all things, "so that God may be all in all" (1 Cor 15:28). The author of the letter to the Colossians expresses that idea by writing that in Christ Jesus, "in [whom] all the fullness of God was pleased to dwell" (Col 1:19), "all things hold together" (Col 1:17).

The goal of total transfiguration has not yet been achieved, but Paul presses on "to make it [his] own, because Christ Jesus has made [him] his own" (Phil 3:12). The NABRE captures the meaning of this verse in an excellent manner. Paul is quoted as writing, "It is not that I have already taken hold of [the resurrection from the dead] or have already attained perfect maturity, but I continue my pursuit in hope that I may possess it, since I have indeed been taken possession of by Christ [Jesus]" (Phil 3:12). To be taken possession of by Christ Jesus is to be transfigured.

The goal of these reflections on being transfigured by silence is not to be exhaustive. Before Paul, Moses was changed by light and the voice of God (Exod 3:2–12); the prophet Isaiah was transfigured by the Lord's light and voice (Isa 6:6–8); the prophet Ezekiel was altered by the LORD's light and voice (Ezek 1:2–28ab). Silent visions of the divine presence transfigure those who see the light and hear the sound of the sheer silence of the voice addressing them.

SACRED
SILENCE PLEASE

Application

Through the use of Scripture, reflection, journaling/meditating, and prayer, the silence that transfigures occurs and the person grows in spirituality; a stronger connection between spirit and Spirit takes place. Once transfigured, we begin to be aware of the divine presence being everywhere—not just in philosophical or theological discourse, but in daily experiences. God is present in each breath, wherever you are sitting or standing, in whatever room you are, on whatever beach you are, or in whatever forest you are. Everyone and everything flashes the light of the divine presence—of course it always did; you just weren't transfigured by silence in order to see it. To be able to hear the sound of sheer silence is a transfiguring experience. All such experiences are tastes of the divine and simultaneously portals to what the fullness of transfiguring will be once we cross over death. Once overcome by the divine presence through transfiguring silence (or animals,[11] trees,[12] or wine[13]), we are changed, never to be the same again because we are one with the divine forever while on the third planet from the sun and whatever is on the other side of death.

Transfiguration through silence is a call to theosis—deification. God's nature, essence, or being is radically incapable of being captured by ordinary language. Ordinary concepts fail utterly. Yet God has made his presence known in silence and awakened us to its transfiguring ability. Life is transformed for here and for hereafter. God shows up and reveals his presence in ordinary human experience, like silence, that transfigures us. If we are aware and not asleep, we recognize the divine presence that sustains all. Once we are transfigured by silence, other realizations begin to occur: According to Garvey, "we wait for God's will to be revealed—usually,

---

11. See *An Abecedarian of Animal Spirit Guides: Spiritual Growth through Reflections on Creatures*, Mark G. Boyer, Wipf and Stock, 2016.

12. See *An Abecedarian of Sacred Tress: Spiritual Growth through Reflections on Woody Plants*, Mark G. Boyer, Wipf and Stock, 2016.

13. See *Fruit of the Vine: A Biblical Spirituality of Wine*, Mark G. Boyer, Wipf and Stock, 2017.

though not always, in silence."[14] According to Shapiro, quoted by Rohr, everything we see, think, feel, and imagine is part of and never apart from the same Source, which is named God, Reality, Brahman, Allah, One, Krishna, the Absolute, etc. While the list of names is long, the reality to which they all point is the same.[15] According to Romano Guardini, quoted by Rohr, God is the creator and we are the creature. Although we are not God, we are not other than God either. Although we are not the earth, we are not other than the earth either.[16] Once transfiguration has occurred, our contemplation swirls with the awareness of how "all things hold together" (Col 1:17) "so that God may be all in all" (1 Cor 15:28). My spirit and your spirit are destined to be Spirit. Silence transfigures spirit into Spirit.

14. Garvey, *Wonder*, 15.

15. Rohr, "Perennial Tradition."

16. Rohr, "Unitive Consciousness."

Bibliography

Boyer, Mark G. *Divine Presence: Elements of Biblical Theophanies*. Eugene, OR: Wipf and Stock, 2017.

Garvey, John. *Only Wonder Comprehends*. Edited by Patrick Jordan. Collegeville, MN: Liturgical, 2018.

John Paul II. "*Rosarium Virginis Mariae*: On the Most Holy Rosary." In *The Liturgy Documents: Volume 4: Supplemental Documents for Parish Worship, Devotion, Formation, and Catechesis*, 525–550. Chicago: Liturgy Training, 2013.

"Meister Eckhart." www.AZQuotes.com/quote/836115.

New American Bible Revised Edition, The. Totowa, NJ: Catholic Book, 2010.

O'Day, Gail R., and David Peterson, eds. *The Access Bible: New Revised Standard Version with the Apocryphal/Deuterocanonical Books*. New York: Oxford University Press, 1999.

Petersen, Meggen Watt. "Working to Stay Here: An Interview with Mirabi Bush." *Spirituality and Health* 21:5 (2018) 60–64.

Rohr, Richard. "Ascending and Descending Religions." *The Mendicant* 8:3 (2018) 1–2.

———. "Perennial Tradition." The Center for Action and Contemplation. August 4, 2018. http://www.cac.org.

———. "Unitive Consciousness." The Center for Action and Contemplation. August 22, 2018. http://www.cac.org.

Scobey, Annmarie. "Keep Prayer in Mind." *U.S. Catholic* 83:5 (2018) 43–44.

Shapiro, Rami. "Roadside Assistance for the Spiritual Traveler." *Spirituality and Health* 21:5 (2018) 19–20.

Thurman, Howard. *Meditations of the Heart*. Boston: Beacon, 1953.

Recent Books by Mark G. Boyer

Nature Spirituality: Praying with Wind, Water, Earth, Fire

A Spirituality of Ageing

Caroling through Advent and Christmas: Daily Reflections with Familiar Hymns

Weekday Saints: Reflections on Their Scriptures

Human Wholeness: A Spirituality of Relationship

The Liturgical Environment: What the Documents Say (third edition)

A Simple Systematic Mariology

Praying Your Way through Luke's Gospel and the Acts of the Apostles

Daybreaks: Daily Reflections for Advent and Christmas

Daybreaks: Daily Reflections for Lent and Easter

An Abecedarian of Animal Spirit Guides: Spiritual Growth through Reflections on Creatures

Overcome with Paschal Joy: Chanting through Lent and Easter— Daily Reflections with Familiar Hymns

Taking Leave of Your Home: Moving in the Peace of Christ

A Spirituality of Mission: Reflections for Holy Week and Easter

An Abecedarian of Sacred Trees: Spiritual Growth through Reflections on Woody Plants